I0409585

Terrorist

University

How Did It Happen That The

U.S. Government Knew

About The Madrid Bombing

And Did Nothing?

2nd Updated and Edited Version

Copyright 2012, by Nicholas Black

All rights reserved. No part of this publication may be reproduced, stored in a retrieval system, or transmitted, in any form or by any means, electronic, mechanical, photocopying, recording, or otherwise, without the prior written permission of the publisher. Printed in the United States of America. For information and inquiries, address Enoch Press at www.EnochPress.com.

Cover Design: Endless Leadz
Editor: Thomas Sliva

Enoch Press books are available at special discounts for bulk purchases in the U.S. by corporations, institutions, and other organizations. For more information, please contact the Special Markets Department at the Enoch Press office via email info@EnochPress.com or via phone at 877-245-6782

Author's note:

I have chosen to slightly alter some names, but for the most part, the people you read about really exist. Alive or dead, they're real people. Real soldiers and terrorists and arms dealers and mercenaries.

Also, Even though nobody called me Huck until I entered the legion, you'll sometimes see it appear earlier to keep things easier to understand. All this name swapping has me confused sometimes, so I can only imagine a reader trying to figure it out.

Thank you for purchasing my book. Please *REVIEW* this book on Amazon. I need your feedback to make the next version better. Thank you so much!

Check out my website where you can download all the evidence at www.TerroristUniversity.com

Table of Contents

HUCK'S WAR

American intelligence had advance knowledge of planned al Qaeda terrorist attacks, including the Madrid Train bombing on 3/11/2004, and did nothing to stop them.

How do I know this?

Because I was a fellow prisoner and close friend of several high-ranking al Qaeda operatives inside the high-security wing of Valdemoro Prison in Spain. This prison has a nickname.

They call it, *"Terrorist University."*

I was asked, and agreed, to participate in an intelligence gathering operation that produced this and other information. My nom de guerre from the French Foreign Legion was Jayden Roy Huck, and this is my story.

PREFACE

WHAT you will read in the following pages may bother you.

It is meant to tell the true account of a poorly run undercover operation that took place between October 2002 and June of 2003. I have kept the true names of the different individuals. However, when dealing with certain individuals who are still at-large, I chose to use only first names.

This is neither an indictment nor an accusation about U.S. governmental and foreign policies when dealing with international terrorism, yet it is critical when appropriate. As the writer, I do not claim to be able to create a literary work that will be appreciated for its eloquent prose. Hey, I carried a pistol before I ever picked up a pen. You might be offended by what you read. Fair enough. It is a true story, and life is often times an offensive string of circumstances.

Every conversation is as accurate as my memory will allow.

Every account is verifiable through evidence in my possession. Yes, I made copies. No, I won't tell you who has them.

Before this all started, when I was still liked by my country, there was a prayer that I stumbled across that I felt best summed up my morality.

SAVIOR

Give me, God, what you still have,

Give me what no one asks for;

I do not ask for wealth

nor for success,

nor even health—

People ask you so often, God, for all that

That you cannot have any left.

Give me, God what you still have;

Give me what people refuse to accept from you.

I want insecurity and disquietude,

I want turmoil and brawl,

And if you should give them to me, my God, once and

for all.

Let me be sure to have them always,

for I will not always have the courage

To ask you for them.

(Zirnheld)

ONE: Especially Bad

I'm not asking for forgiveness – that's something between God and me. And lately, He's been pretty quiet.

There's something you should know about me: I'm not one of the good guys. Often I'm quick tempered. My moral compass spins in every direction. I like the attractive girls first, and if they end up with a personality – so be it. I like to fight. Most times I'm no more than three feet away from a pistol. As far as my personality, well, I don't really have one.

I'm a kind of messed-up mixture of every character I've ever seen on film, television, cartoons, or comic books. I lack any real identity, and I blame nobody. That's what made me a good spy.

I remember, back in the early nineties, watching television one time and seeing them break from the regular programming with coverage of some accident that had occurred at the World Trade Center. I remember sketchy images of thick pitch-black smoke pouring out of the side of the parking garage like a volcano had erupted. It looked like a bad Hollywood effect.

They weren't sure what specifically had happened, but it was not *natural.* That kind of carnage rarely is. Religious violence is one of those neat things that we humans gave to the world.

A couple of days later, information started leaking out that perhaps this was not an *accident* as it was first reported. No – this was something foreign to us – something different.

This was the first successful act of terrorism against the United States of America inside the invisible barriers of our country that we all think are there. Everybody started saying that America was lucky that it had taken this long. That seemed a rather odd assertion of luck. The talking-heads preached about how we had pushed the envelope for so long with our foreign policy, and so far with our imperialistic mentality, that it was just a matter of *when* and not *if.*

I was just out of high school at the time, and I didn't really consider it all that much. Terrorism was something that Arab people do because they hate their jobs and the weather is too hot in the Middle East. I didn't really care much about politics. The most American spirit I had was when I watched the Olympics for about fifteen minutes every couple of years to see if an American was going to win anything – and mostly I was disappointed with that too. Youth and wisdom are usually more like sparring partners than lovers walking hand-in-hand.

I pretty much just did my own thing, and like most Americans, didn't pay much attention to those *extremists.* To most of us, terrorism was not an issue, but just a bunch of immature adolescents vying for attention. It was best just to treat them like an annoying child who is running around at a birthday party with his pants down. Ignore it. Surely *they* would fade off into the distance soon enough. Then our lives could just go back to the comfortable average we are all so used to.

The unfortunate thing about my rather negligent attitude towards terrorism is that I wasn't the only one who had this mentality. Apparently the FBI, CIA, local and state authorities, and all of the other people that are charged with keeping us safe shared it. Those other people with the same level of disregard and apathy, maybe, shouldn't have been so indifferent to the very clear threats that were knocking on our door.

I distinctly remember, during one of my long talks with a high-ranking member of al Qaeda, him saying "this apathy and arrogance were among the reasons it was so easy to attack America. America was a 'me, me, me society.' You let us do this," he said.

You let us do this.

This was a rather ominous statement coming from a man wanted by ten different countries for acts of terrorism, arms trafficking, bomb making, and the list goes on and on, and a man whose last roommate was Illich Ramirez Sanchez, (otherwise known as "Carlos the Jackal.") You might wonder how I ever got involved with one of al Qaeda's top men. It's an interesting story that will probably leave you a little angry, a bit paranoid, but most of all – disappointed. I'm not political. I'm not trying to make a statement. I'm not a harbinger of bad news or twisted philosophy. Maybe I'll be dead by the time anyone ever reads this. And if I'm not dead, I'll be a nobody – just another number in the machine.

I'm not special in any way. I'm just a bad guy who infiltrated al Qaeda deeper than any other American had. Regardless of what you've heard about the education of a spook – it takes a bad guy like me to do what I did.

Maybe I am *special*.

Especially bad.

TWO: Empire Building

"That guy ain't your buddy," Dan said.

"And he ain't gonna give you nothing." Dan looked at me with deep brown eyes, his face tanned partly from the sun, and partly from his Cuban blood. "Go out there and fuck that dude up! Shut this crowd up," he said as we walked toward the ring. There might have been 4,000 people waiting to see their hometown boy kick my ass.

We were in McAllen, Texas for a full contact, mixed martial arts fight. I had three and a half years of college under my belt, had gotten out of the US Navy, and was making money as a fighter/bodyguard/door guy. But you have to build up a reputation. So here I was, taking this fight for a couple hundred bucks. Truth be known, I'd have fought for free. Normally, I'd be choking out drunks at some bar I worked at for 10 bucks an hour. So actually, this was much safer. There were no beer bottles in the ring.

Dan, my trainer and friend, was also an agent with the U.S. Treasury Department. He was an investigator for CID (Criminal Investigation Division), (You know, the guys who got Al Capone.) Anyway, he and I did stuff together all the time – fighting, shooting, surveillance, womanizing – good healthy fun!

Dan said, as we're almost to the edge of the ring, "Be like those animals that go crazy on the Discovery Channel!"

"When Animals Attack?" I answered with a lifeless grin creeping out the side of my face.

"That's the one," he said. If you pay close attention, you can tell that Dan is from some Latin country where the drinking age is twelve, and traffic cops have machine guns and beards. The accent swims underneath the surface of his words like an eel.

Fifty-one seconds later I was walking away from the ring.

The crowd was silent. This was a bad scene in a B-movie.

The guy I fought was lying unconscious from a triangle leg choke, and the referee, Tito Ortiz, was trying to revive him. I've only ever seen that many people be that quiet one other time in my life. Anyway, that was my first pro fight.

I wasn't the best fighter, but I wasn't getting my ass kicked either. I had trained with some very talented Brazilians to learn my ground fighting and with a perpetually irate Thai to learn my kickboxing. Dan filled in the gaps. At the time, I didn't speak Portuguese, Thai, or Spanish, so I didn't really know what they were saying most of the time, although "Stupid American!" was easy enough to understand. After five professional fights and several pit-fights, I had two world championship belts and some extra cash. It wasn't a career, but it was good enough for the time being.

In all, I had most of those fights before I started getting into trouble.

With the fighting came some opportunities as a bodyguard for notoriety. That brought all sorts of people. I worked for some actors, some businessmen, some musicians, and, on occasion, a few mob guys, (Hey, you go where the money is.)

Anyway, in 1997, I gave an old friend a ride out to this small town so he could deliver some steroids to some guy he didn't really trust. He wanted me to drive him out there, give him a little back up. (What the hell, right?) Of course, the whole thing turned out to be a sting operation aimed at eradicating the *Steroid Menace.*

I found this out while sitting alone in my car waiting for my friend. A bunch of guys started falling out of this car that pulled up about twenty yards in front of my car in a Wal-Mart parking lot. I pulled my pistol, an H&K USP 9mm, but when I saw the police vests and heard them yelling "Police," I placed the pistol back down beside the seat and waited with my hands on the steering wheel.

(I'm not going to get into a shootout with a bunch of cops. Besides, from a tactical standpoint, I'd probably only get three or four of them before they made Swiss cheese out of my ass. Ok, as clumsy as they were, I might have taken five, but that's neither here nor there. Most cops aren't *shooters*, and I wouldn't expect them to be.)

So now, I'm a felon with the social stigma and all that goes with that. I did 320 hours of community service teaching federal agents and cops how to kick the asses of people like me. In a way, that's kind of funny. I lost my car; they fined me $3,500; they made me report to this nice old lady in Dallas who explained to me that if I stayed out of trouble and completed my probation, I would be able to get the case dropped, and then I'd get a clean record back. But, you know – people like me can never just go straight down a road. We always have to swerve around the slower traffic, even if it means putting a couple of the slower cars in a ditch along the way.

Next, I start body guarding this guy named Tony. He has this internet company that is going to make everybody rich. At that time, in 2000, everybody was making so much money on the Internet – *Dot com! Dot com!* – that if somebody was into an IPO or something – you didn't ask questions, you just threw money at them.

At the time I was making about 20 K a month setting up all of the different security aspects and procedures for Tony's company, Stadtt Media LLC. Tony pulls me aside one day and asks me to go to a gun show and get some guns for the *guys* to shoot at the range. By *guys* he meant any of the board of directors, programmers, V.P.'s, etc. – toys for the upwardly mobile to play with. I didn't think much of it. In the previous months I had purchased go-carts, radio controlled cars, and prostitutes. One night we spent about 40 K at a strip bar. So, no – the thought of spending a bunch of investors' money didn't bother me. I figured that everybody was going to be so *crazy rich*, (Tony's term), that it wouldn't matter. He hands me 20, 30 K and I'm on my way. I call a guy, who knows a guy. Next thing I know, there's a gun-dealer buddy of mine taking my cash and turning it into guns.

So, months and months go by and everything is cool. Tony's company is doing just swell; everyone's talking about how rich the investors are going to be. "Just like Microsoft," they would say. But no! This was no Microsoft, because at Microsoft they don't hire a douche bag con artist as their head stockbroker.

Well, Tony did, and let's call him Rob. This idiot broker, Rob, made some statements in the company's prospectus that violated several SEC rules – enough, in fact, to get the company's assets frozen and thrown into receivership.

So now, not only does nobody get paid anymore, but all of our stock is now frozen. It cannot be traded in any capacity. My security company had around 1.5 million shares of Stadtt Media – 1.5 million shares of nothing!

And the dream is dead.

Well, when the well runs dry, you don't sit around sad and thirsty. No, you move on to the next gig, (You know, Soldier for hire), and all that.

Next, I get hooked up with a restaurant company and help set up some security scenarios, risk management, etc. – I trade in my pistol for a tie and some Versace.

A year now goes by without incident – then one night I get a call from Tony. He says that he wants a "can," which in our terms is a silencer. I tell him "I can't get one," which really, is a big fat lie. On the phone he's sounding like a freakin' coked-out psychopath, so I decide that it would be in society's best interest if I didn't act on the request. (Besides, he still owed me more than 30 grand, so I wouldn't be doing any more free back flips – and fat chance on ever seeing any of that cash.)

After this call, I decide that I had better make sure that Tony couldn't get access to any of the other weapons. At this point they were locked securely away in a gun safe. I got my Fed buddy, Dan, on the phone and asked him to come and take possession of the weapons (four in all). He agreed. Two hours later he presented the rifles to the ATF, and that was the last I heard of it – until the Federal Government indicted me – lots of cops, guns, and matching silver bracelets.

So I ended up locked-up, sitting in a federal detention center. They didn't want to let me out on bond because they said I'm dangerous. Then, just to put a cherry on top, they give the judge some song and dance about me being a flight risk. (Who, little old me – a flight risk?)

Apparently, I had violated federal law when I attended the Gun show, and helped facilitate the original gun purchase. As I still had a felony, (it had not yet been dropped from my record), the recent activity made me a "Felon in Possession of a Firearm." This was not a crime for which I would have to go to prison, however, there was just one catch. I would have to testify against Tony, and other people who worked at Stadtt Media, even my Fed buddy, Dan.

As it so strangely turned out, Tony was wanted for a *murder for hire* conspiracy that had occurred on the East Coast, long before we ever met him. The Fed's believed that I, being a close confidant of Tony, would have heard about this *murder* – loose talk among friends, or something like that. Anyway, they said if I would just testify to all that, I would get probation, or some minor penalty.

At the exact same time, Dan was being investigated by Internal Affairs for some nonsense about leaking sensitive information, and they wanted me to testify against him, too. The real beef on that was – because he was a Cuban American who was involved in a lawsuit against the IRS, he should have made his next pay grade long ago, and for some odd reason, none of the Hispanic agents had been given their promotions.

Can you say, "Class Action?" Well, the promotion snub would have severely quieted their legal action. This was the time honored *Good old boy* system in action.

When presented with all of this, I was a bit dumbfounded.

They surrounded me with about 15 or 20 agents to take me in, even though I had never made any attempt to run or hide, or even elude the authorities. They never contacted my attorney, nor asked me to come in. Then, they tell me that I *know* all of this stuff – how, being as close as I was to Tony, I must have seen and heard things important to this investigation. The Assistant District Attorney even went so far as to present a page of typed information for me to *familiarize* myself with. On the page were things that I didn't know, wasn't familiar with, and could not have possibly been party to. The entire time, my attorney is all smiles, and nods, and says "can I get you a cup of coffee Mr. Prosecutor?" He was scared to death of these Feds, and he'd have cut off one of his two faces to get out of that federal building. In a nutshell, they wanted me to be their star witness and perjure myself testifying to a bunch of stuff I never knew, or could never have known.

So, for about a trillion reasons, I had made up my mind what to do.

I was facing prison time and fines. I would forever be vilified as a *convict*. I was on "Death Ground" as the Samurai say. I had to make a choice and whatever that was – it was one of those "no turning back now" kind of decisions.

A federal case is a lot like a virulent disease that has infected your foot. It is coming, and there's no stopping its path of destruction. It isn't a choice of how to cure the disease – unless you're a grass (rat). No, it's more like *cut off the leg to save the body.*

I informed them that I needed time outside to prepare for court. They said that the only way I'd be eligible for a bond would be if I pled guilty to one (1) count of "Felon in Possession of a Firearm." The fact that I was never found with a gun of any kind is apparently immaterial in Federal Court. So, I gave them one of those toothless smiles and pled guilty. I told them I would show up for trial and be a good little boy. They granted me bond and told me to get ready to testify.

I was informed that I should stay nearby, (as in the state of Texas.) I did a lot of nodding and smiling, thank you so much, blah, blah, blah. The day I hit the street, I started selling everything that I owned. I was getting *liquid.*

The timing of all of this was right around September 11th, 2001. People were absolutely batty about travel and flying. I would use this to my advantage. One of my partners, Niles, decided that he didn't want to participate in the government's nonsense either, so he informed me that he would be coming with me. We raised about 50 grand in all, paid off as many debts as we could, kissed our girlfriends one last time and left on Thanksgiving weekend . . . for Mexico.

We disappeared into central Mexico for a while, and then left Mexico City on January 1st, non-stop service to Paris, France. We got off of the plane at Charles De Gaulle Airport and made our way, through the freezing slush and snow, to the front gate of *Fort De Nogent.* This was the place where people on the run might end up if they wanted to join the French Foreign Legion . . . and that's exactly what we did.

It was lovely. We were doing a very difficult training course for commandos. We were getting the piss kicked out of us by the instructors, who were themselves criminals on the run from other countries (mostly Russia and the other eastern-bloc countries).

Everyone around us was bad – criminals, murderers, ex-spies from KGB, Mossad, and soldiers-for-hire. So, we felt proud to be among such reputable amigos.

Truth is, it was a bloody den of killers, psychopaths, and lunatics. (But then, the Legion Étrangère is a small military – 8,500 soldiers – who are all trained to create the highest amount of destruction and violence in the shortest amount of time.)

Maximum violence, instantly.

And that's exactly how they trained us. We were basically put through a Guerrilla Warfare program for seven months.

(The Legionnaire is probably the toughest soldier in the world, though perhaps not the smartest. They are definitely not the cleanest or most polite, and you probably shouldn't invite them to meet your family or talk politics. They are simply just cold, hard, and mean. Niles and I felt so at home.)

Early on in training I had trashed my left knee pretty good. I think they said that the ACL was completely unattached, and that the Meniscus, as well as the PCL was virtually destroyed. They wanted me to get surgery.

I decided to finish the training before I got cut on.

After our class graduated, I went for surgery and was put on a kind of medical leave/suspension. It meant that I could return when I was ready to get jump (parachute) qualified.

I decided to do my rehab work in Spain. We chose the island of Ibiza, just off of the east coast, in the Balearic Islands. This is one of the most extravagant party islands in the world. Its hedonism personified. Its sex, drugs, decadence, voodoo, knife fights, ghosts, and spirituality in its ugliest forms.

And that's when everything got sideways.

THREE: Welcome to Ibiza

The guys and I arrived on a Thursday afternoon, after having spent 10 or 12 hours on a large ferry ship that had left the night before from Barcelona, Spain. I spent most of the trip sitting near the back of the ship just watching the white foam evaporate into the blackness of the Mediterranean. I was ready for a little recuperation time for my knee, and the time away from loud, violent Legion instructors would be a relaxing change.

But as soon as I got off of the ferry and looked around at all of the excitement, I knew that I was not going to get anything even approaching quiet on that island. The thump of hard house music was almost constantly heard from any place on the island. Every restaurant, shopping center, club, bar, or gas station was jumping to the beat.

The next thing that a person would instantly notice is the amount of ethnic diversity on the island – Spanish, Russians, English, Americans, Moroccans, French, Portuguese, Irish, Senegalese, and more. There is every color of skin, style of hair, and type of accent you could possibly imagine, and everyone gets along quite well. There are so many beautiful girls that it was difficult to focus on much else.

First things first: We contacted a real estate guy, Anthony 'el Santo', or 'the Saint,' as we called him later. He found us an apartment in Sant Antoni, Ibiza, located on the southern tip of the island that would cost us about 1,200 euros a month. From the apartment we could see the water, the gym, and the clubs. We were near enough to a shopping center that we didn't need a vehicle. We would just use buses, taxis, and our feet to get wherever we needed to go. (And really, you don't need that much to survive on a small party island like Ibiza.)

Within the week, the Saint had introduced us to several club owners, and we found work as door-guys. It was decent cash, about 400 *quid* (pound sterling) a week. It was more than enough to pay the bills and concentrate on training. In our spare time we set up a security consulting company that would do almost anything that you wanted us to do. Hey . . . we're mercenaries, right?

And that, my friends, is how *5 Commando* was born. Our company, 5 Comm, would handle any security concern you could possibly dream up. Why '5'? Well, there were five of us, we were commandos, and it was paying a bit of tribute to Mr. Denard – a French soldier-for-hire who was the subject of much mercenary lore.

So we did some bodyguard gigs here and there. We did a couple of feasibility studies, which is basically just breaking into a facility and then reporting to the owners how they might fix their security to deal with undesirables like ourselves. We did a few jobs, made some cash, and started to put together a good little crew. Everything was going about just fine – that is, until the sword fight.

At one of the clubs where we were working, these two Arab men started fighting. Now, normally, two people fighting in the street is no big deal; it happens all the bloody time. But in this case, one of the guys was carrying a small sword. I'm not embellishing. No, it wasn't a large knife. Rambo had a knife. It was most certainly a sword. It made that *wheew* sound when he swung it at the other guy's face. I should have just sat back and enjoyed the show, but the cops were coming from up the street, and I didn't want these guys getting arrested. (I'd rather kill a guy than give him to the cops.) My buddy Cael and I cautiously approached the men, and in our most polite and respectful way, tried to tell them that the policia were headed this way! They both split up and the cops chased them. It was all very fun. I saw the sword get thrown in a small landscaped area around the side. Cael and I both decided not to tell the cops where the sword was. Both of those Arab men were detained but later released.

A couple of nights later, the Arab man who had been wielding the sword came and thanked me for not grassing (ratting, snitching, etc.) him up to the policia. These policia had been local cops – Guardia Civil – and had decided to release the Arab men without charges being filed. One Arab was very polite and explained to me that anything he could do for me would be his pleasure. Well, being on the run as I was, I decided to ask him about a passport. He said that it would take a couple of weeks, but that he'd get back to me. We traded cell phone numbers, and that was that.

Two days later I got a call to meet him down at a Moroccan bar. Outside, in his Mercedes, he showed me about 10 or 15 passports from France, Spain, England, and I think there may have even been a Canadian or two. He then told me that they were easy to get because the policia were selling them to him and the other *Brothers* for next to nothing. They (him and the brothers) were then getting pictures of the people who wanted passports and sending them all off to France where some artist would insert the new photos into the passports. Voila! Now Joe Terrorista becomes Johnny English with entry into almost every country in the free world, including the United States.

He also explained to me that he would be able to get travelers checks that were stolen, and then doctor them up so that they could be used again. He was giving 30 cents on the euro for those or selling them for half price. He could also get drivers' licenses and other supporting documents. That was how he did for all of the Brothers that were coming up from Morocco, Lebanon, Algeria, Tunisia, Egypt, Libya, and the list goes on.

To tell you honestly, I still don't know why he decided to confide in me all of this. It seemed like a huge security risk. I mean, we were barely a year after 9/11. Anyway, I handed him some photos of me and decided to see what he could produce. He said he'd call me, and we split.

Something about all of this didn't sit well with me. I'm a bad guy and all, but I don't kill innocent people. Terrorists seem not to have a problem with non-combatant casualties, and if you're making moves for a bunch of would be terrorists, then . . . you're a terrorist too.

I decided to make a call to an old friend. He knew some people at the CIA, and they were more than a bit interested. Unfortunately, they wanted me to fly out to Barcelona and meet the Station Chief at the embassy. Now, you see, I'm still on the run.

Well, I'm not a genius, but I think they'd have just loved to take me into custody right then and there. So I politely declined his offer and told him to call me when they decided what course of action they were going to take.

I didn't hear anything for a couple of days. After, I was working at the club, and something strange happened. Approached by two Americans, they presented black *Diplomatic* passports to me to get into the club. At first, thinking they are trying to see if they can get a rise out of me, I deliberately said something to the other door guy in Spanish and handed him the passports. He then nodded and let them into the club. They were probably inside for twenty minutes or so before they came back out and hung out at the door.

I guess that some company (CIA) guys are good operators, but most of the ones that I've met were clueless morons. You can't take a kid out of Harvard or Yale, and then make him a spook in six months. As far as I know, the only good spies left are English, Russian, French, or Israeli. American spies throw cash around for a week, and then take down a target – lots of press; lots of nonsense.

I was waiting for the moment where they might say that they were here to take me into custody or something. (But then – who the hell am I? It's not like I'm public enemy number one. I went to a freakin' gun show and caught an indictment.) After a couple of minutes, one of them told me that they work for the state department, and that they would be interested if I knew anything about Middle Eastern men on the island doing anything strange or out of place.

The thing about Ibiza is that nothing is taboo or out of place. But that being said, I figured that they had been sent by the embassy in Barcelona, and that they probably were trying to do some good.

I still had a patriotic flame burning a bit inside me. Not a fire, mind you, but I still believed in what America stood for. I guess I figured that if I helped, it would make my most heinous 'crimes' seem a little less awful when compared to the bigger picture. I would help them.

I told them that I had seen some things that could be related to the security of our borders. They then conveyed to me that they were very interested in what I had to say. They told me that they'd be in touch, (whatever that's supposed to mean.)

They never explained how they were going to contact me, exactly. We didn't exchange numbers or anything clever like that. (But then, this is the CIA – so I'm sure they have all sorts of incredibly brilliant methods which commoners like myself can't possibly imagine.) So I nodded. They nodded. And that was that.

I went back down to the club where I had originally met the passport-sword-guy. I figured I'd do a little pre-op recon. I decided to take a couple of notes: make some rough maps on the location, and some other tactical notes (entry into the building, access, egress, perimeter, etc. – the kind of stuff that spooks would eventually have to do if they were going to hit the place.) After doing this I memorized what I could, coded the rest, and then destroyed the original notes.

I then made a list of the items that I would need to be provided by the spooks to properly do my job: digital camera, satellite-secure phone or burst transmitter, small caliber pistol that can be silenced, portable recording device, chewing gum that turns into high-explosive. (Well, that last one didn't make the final list.)

You may wonder why I thought they might want to use me to do their dirty work. I would love to tell you that it was because I'm trained commando with experience in the intelligence field, or that I spoke four of five languages, or because I was a world champion mixed martial arts fighter, or even that I was just a cleverly placed insider that had already established rapport with the bad guys. But no, none of that was the reason. It was more like plausible deniability. In their eyes, if I get caught, I'm just some rogue convict on the run from the U.S. Government. They'd probably even spin it that I was working for the bad guys in some capacity. But it wouldn't come out that it was a sanctioned Op on foreign soil being run without the express permission of the Spanish Government, (not that the US is known for asking permission.)

Regardless, I was in the right place and to position another agent or asset could take months, if not longer, or it might not have even been possible. When you're dealing with the immigration of terrorists every day, your loss is another potential 9/11.

But then they did something very surprising; a move that was so genius that I couldn't have possibly predicted it.

FOUR: Ever been to a Spanish Prison?

"Hi," my name is Jayden R. Huck, and I am a bad guy." That sounds like my opening line at some Mercenaries Anonymous meeting, but it is the truth.

At this point in the story, you, the reader, know how I got into trouble. You know that I went on the run and ended up in the French Foreign Legion, but you're still not sure about this whole spy business.

The brilliant move that the government made was to arrest me. It happened while I was entering the gym that I trained at regularly. The gym was located on the south end of the island overlooking the Mediterranean. I was just inside the door when a group of agents from both the Spanish Federales and INTERPOL tackled me and my buddy Paul.

They got me in front of a judge who said that I would be shipped back to the United States because I was considered a very dangerous person – Yeah, heard all that before. They asked if I wanted to fight against extradition (for example: those claiming political refugee status). I said that I should probably go back to the U.S. and face the music. They then threw me in a dark room for a couple of days. They bounced me around a couple of local jails in Ibiza, and then I caught a chaperoned flight to

Valencia. Next thing I knew, I was getting what we call *diesel therapy.* That is when they put you in a new prison every couple of days – between your long, extended, superfluous bus rides.

I ended up in Madrid at a prison with the name Valdemoro, but to police agencies and the local populous, it is known affectionately as "Terrorist University."

They say that there are more terrorists per-square-foot inside those prison walls than in any other prison on Earth. This is taking into consideration Camp X-ray, at Guantanamo bay, and all of those 'secret' prisons that the CIA allegedly runs. The people at Valdemoro are real live bad guys. The kind of people who will, without hesitation, kill you and everybody you're associated with if it fits their needs. These guys aren't all religiously motivated either. The Muslim fundamentalists are only a small portion of the harbingers of violence.

Included in the list, you have the Basque Separatists – who blow up cars and senators all the time in Spain, because they want their small state's autonomy (which is about the size of a farm).

Then there is the Italian Red Brigade – a group of fire-loving Fascists, hoping for some new phantom government that will save Italy.

The French are so confusing with their bomb-makers, gangsters, and religious zealots that I won't even delve into them.

Let us not forget the fall of communism, which marked the end of the Cold War and the beginning of a new era in eastern-bloc psychopathology. Tons of gangs – some of them Mafia, rebel factions, ex-military, gunrunners, hit men, continue on ad nauseam.

The Moroccans have their own drug cartels – The Senegalese, The Belge, The Pakistanis, and The Lebanese. Throw in the whole of North Africa as well – I know your eyes are rolling, but the list goes on – The English and Irish. (Well, of course you know about all that.)

Anyway, almost every terrorist group, gang, faction, front, syndicate, or association has representatives in Valdemoro. Some of them are dangerous because of their religious underpinnings, but mostly it's the latent European Capitalism rearing its ugly head here. The lust for money is greed in its purest form.

So the bad guys in Valdemoro are for real. If somebody talks slick to somebody important, they get appropriately dealt with, and in a timely manner.

As far as these gangs' business connections are concerned, being on the inside of a Spanish prison makes no difference; it's just another work day. In the Spanish facilities they allow real money (euros.) (I'm not exactly sure what the theory was on that.) Three hundred euros to a functionario (prison guard) and you can get anything that can be smuggled in. You just get your people on the outside to put a package together and deliver it to the functionario, and your prize will arrive in a day. Italians guys were ordering Algerian hits, written in Arabic and smuggled out of the prison through one of the Spanish language teachers. We had cellular phones, drugs, and women on the weekends. We wore our own clothes, had jewelry, and Play stations, and there was a 24-7 black market.

So I'm with all these real-live bad guys, and for the first time, I realize that if these guys ever got organized – well, then everyone in the free world was going to have some real problems.

I kept my head down for a few days and checked everyone out. I decided that I could trust this English guy named James. He had been a quite talented goalie for a semi-pro football club until he found that drug smuggling was much more lucrative. Along the way he accidentally killed a couple of people, (typical, really.) So he was the guy who introduced me to the prison's *collection* guys. They were all eastern-bloc, mostly Russian and Polish mob that collected all of the outstanding debts owed by other prisoners. As it turned out, the first call I was able to make was courtesy of the Russians – it was on a smuggled cell phone, to my attorney.

He told me that he'd been on a plane, and that the State Department had been talking to him. Isn't that an interesting coincidence? Perhaps my arrest was not so accidental.

My attorney arrived three days later to ask me all sorts of things about passports, travelers checks, and terrorists. During our meeting, through a glass wall, he did not ask me one question about my legal situation. He informed me that he had been sent to get information so that the US and Spanish could go after these *terrorist enablers*. He also asked me if I was aware that they had

14 or 15 alleged al Qaeda suspects that just so happened to be in the same prison I was in – I knew where this was leading.

He wondered if, since I spoke French and was such a personable mercenary, if I could get *in* with these guys. Why French? Well, most of the Middle East speaks French. And these particular suspects, who were Algerian, Egyptian, and Saudi – probably wouldn't suspect a guy like me to be a spook.

(Oh, yeah – and I'd be the one getting killed if it all went tits-up, not him.)

Anyway, he half asked me and half told me to try to do this. This appealed to my patriotic nature. Before I could answer, he told me that there were guys at the State Department, as well as NIS (Naval Investigative Service) that were interested in how close I could get to the 'AQ Boys' as they were later dubbed. I just shrugged. (What the hell, right?)

So he told me to keep in touch, communicate every couple of days, and try not to get killed while hunting for Osama. "Cheers, mate – Best of luck to you!"

Two days later I heard my name being butchered on the intercom. I headed through the high-security facility towards one of the many electrically controlled gates that herd the prisoners like cattle to and fro. They pointed at me from behind thick glass and bars, and said "visita, visita." (Another interesting note: The prison guards do not enter population with the inmates. They were always behind a glass-enclosed area where you couldn't get to them.) So the men behind the glass were pointing toward the large corridor that is like a main artery to all of the areas of the prison. (I thought, "hmmm . . . that's odd," because my attorney was supposed to be back in the states by now.) I was curious what he wanted. But when I arrived at the glass wall, I saw two guys that looked like Feds.

There's a difference between Feds (federal agents on the law enforcement side), and spooks (intelligence agents). Feds dress like cops, act like lawyers, and talk like high school math teachers. Spooks, on the other hand, dress like locals, act like whomever their cover dictates, and talk like your best friend. Now, I'm referring more to your *cold war* spies. Lately the intelligence agencies seem to be turning out cookie-cutter spies who might as well wear t-shirts with *I'm in the CIA* printed on the front and back.

Anyway, these particular two men looked like feds. One of them was tall and dark skinned, with slightly curly hair that didn't understand the effects of gravity. The other guy was a buttoned-down white guy whose appearance seemed to be screaming *accountant!* (You know the type: cheap suit, kind of squirmy.)

The dark one was from INS (Immigration & Naturalization Service), and the second one claimed to be somehow related to INS. I didn't get a business card or get to study their ID's so they could have been anybody. I never got the dark one's name, but the squirmy one said his name was Ted. It was probably short for Theodore. But after talking to them for about twenty seconds, I realized that they were too straight-laced to be spooks, and if they were, well – that pretty much sums up what I've been saying about poorly trained spies and the demise of our intelligence agencies.

They hit me with a barrage of questions about the passport doctoring and smuggling. I told them what I knew about the different locations and players. They took copious notes and then asked if I knew what was going on with my legal situation, and if I would be going back to the island anytime soon. Well, that confirmed that they were not related to the guys at State. It also told me that behind the scenes, there were tons of different agencies trying to get what I had or could give them. That's not very inspiring since they were so bloody incompetent when it came to interagency communication and cooperation.

If you don't believe me, read any page out of the 9/11 Commission's Report – mistake after mistake, then cover-up. For the record, I'm not a conspiracy theorist.

Anyway, they asked me if I could draw a map of the locations that were important. I shrugged to them in the affirmative. They said they'd see what they could do to get me back to Ibiza, but it was not a convincing sell. Truth is, they were done with me the minute I finished giving them their notes. No worries, though – I was already trying to figure out how to infiltrate al Qaeda. That's how I stay sharp – one job to the next. I don't like down time, and don't really want it. If you stay in the game, you won't get lazy.

There really isn't any guidebook to being a spy or an *asset* as they sometimes refer. You can learn it one of a few ways. First, you can finish college and then join an intelligence agency. You'll probably need a degree in Political Science, Psychology, or Languages. Then you play their politics and get trained as a field operator. That usually means going to some school in Virginia for a couple of months. When you're done, they'll most likely post you at an embassy or give you to a task force, and good luck with all that.

The second way – my way – is to move around in every circle. That is to say: go to every country you can; live with different people, and learn their different customs and skills. You have to be willing to be good sometimes and bad most times. If you're scared of getting blood or dirt on your hands, then you won't be worth the investment. You need to learn several languages. A former Colonel in the Croatian army told me that, "language is like a weapon", one that people can't take away from you when you're captured – a weapon they don't ever see.

In my opinion, a *real* spy needs to be able to fit into any situation or circumstance. He needs to be equally able to function in high society, as well as the dirtiest, darkest ghettos. He had better be able to fight and have some understanding of unconventional/discretionary/guerrilla warfare. He should know how to talk to and seduce members of the opposite sex. He should have an aptitude for languages. Above all else, he should be able to find solutions to problems that have no solutions, because, basically, if you mess up one time – they're using a HAZMAT team to deal with your *polonium-210* filled body, (or lead, or depleted-uranium, or poison, or – you get the point). You must have total adaptability on the fly.

And all of those things, for better or for worse, I can do.

FIVE: Lock-Down

So here's what I was looking at:

In my modulo (unit) there were about 70 guys. The breakdown was something like this: 8 or 10 Italians, 15 or so Russians and other eastern-bloc gangsters, 8 Basque Separatists, a couple of French, some Columbians, quite a few Spanish, one or two Jamaicans, one Israeli (who I will mention later), and about 8 or 9 middle eastern men (the aforementioned al Qaeda suspects).

James and I were working with the Russians, collecting outstanding debts and stuff like that. I guess I should quickly explain how I got in with them. The Russian guys were big into wrestling around and generally pounding the crap out of each other. I told James that I didn't think there was a one of them who I couldn't choke out. He laughed and then told them about my challenge. It took me about a minute to slap a triangle-leg choke on one of the bigger Russians. He tapped out, and I was in.

So here I am needing to find a way in with the AQ boys, but that was going to be difficult for several reasons. Obviously I couldn't just go over and pick a fight with al Qaeda. For each group, you need a different system.

First, their defenses were about as high up as they could be due to the fact that they were being held as terrorist suspects – probably at the behest of the U.S. Government. They were literally looking for American or Spanish spies that might be attempting to infiltrate their organization.

Strategically placing intelligence agents behind prison walls is an age-old tactic. Sometimes they will have the agents just sit and watch; sometimes they will try to facilitate an operation to entrap the bad guys; and on rare occasions they will even engineer a 'break-out' so that the agent can instantly gain access into the organization by paving the way for their escape. Anyway, such behind-the-wire measures are often used by the various agencies, and bad guys are always on the lookout for such tactics.

The second problem was, in my case, that the AQ boys weren't associating with any of the other inmates accept one, the Israeli – strange bedfellows. Regardless, they all ate together, prayed together, and exercised together.

There was still another hill to climb. Although the media would have us believe that Arabs are dull-witted and daft, the reality is that they are very intelligent; intelligent enough that I wouldn't be able to just go in and sit down with them. Being American, I was already walking around with the scarlet letter. I probably had a huge bull's-eye on my head.

I decided that I needed to do a bit of preliminary maneuvering.

I let it be known, in no uncertain terms, that I was anti-American. The way I approached this was by letting certain people know that I was on the run from the U. S. for being an 'arms dealer,' and that to escape the government, I had joined the

French Foreign Legion. Now, I didn't tell everyone about this, just a few people that I had noticed as being rather social with the other inmates and groups.

Another thing that I decided to do was shoot baskets whenever any of the AQ boys were outside. The units were all self-contained, having a cafeteria, day room, and a recreational area. Our recreational area, referred to as the "rec-yard," was a large concrete square with a couple of goal posts and a basketball rim. Eighteen or twenty-four feet high walls, also made of thick concrete, surrounded the entire area. In our yard there was a large black mark on the outside wall where somebody had thrown a bag full of explosives from outside of the prison somewhere. The wall didn't even buckle. Anyway, I confined my activity to shooting at the basketball rim, in this concrete paradise.

There is a rather common misconception among Europeans that all Americans are good at playing basketball. Well, I defy that by being quite terrible. Ok, I can play defense well enough, and I can shoot from the line; but my outside jumper is garbage, and I can't hit a 3 to save the Pope. So, while the AQ boys were walking around the recreation yard, I was throwing up enough bricks to rebuild the World Trade Center. I would even try to purposely miss so that the ball would bounce over towards them. My theory was that they would feel obligated to retrieve the ball. They were all very polite. One of them would always bring the ball back to me, placing it in my hands very delicately as if he were handling shock-intolerant high explosives. I would nod to him and smile, saying, "Merci, merci." I would then turn and throw up another dud. There are all kinds of ways to establish rapport with people – this was one of mine. It was just a matter of time.

When I wasn't missing shots on the rim, I was sitting quietly at a table in our day room. I would read magazines that I didn't think would be perceived as offensive. You know, no naked girls on the front (National Geographic – yes; Maxim – no). I would also make it a point to be studying Spanish language books, dictionaries, etc. My thinking was that your typical devout Muslim extremist would be perplexed that I wasn't the stereotypical American pig. Anyway, it's all nuance, window dressing so to speak. I just didn't want to give them a reason 'not' to talk to me.

I was outside one day, shooting like Shaquille – not making anything from the free-throw line. As the AQ boys neared me on their orbit around the yard, I nailed one – nothing but net. It was a freakin' sick, sweet nectar, kind of shot! As I went to retrieve the ball, I heard people clapping. I turned around and five or six of them were standing near the free-throw line giving me a golf clap.

In French, I replied humbly, "After only two million times," and I shrugged. They laughed and then continued along their elliptical path throughout the yard. That might not sound like much, but it was breakthrough number one.

The next morning came number two. I was sitting alone for breakfast, just enjoying my little packages of cookies along with some coffee that was so full of milk and sugar that Marlon Brando would have floated in it. As I sat there, minding my own business, Jack came and sat down next to me. He introduced himself and then sat across from me. He offered me some of his cookies and I accepted.

Jack – legal name: Yarrok Asraf – was about 5'9", maybe two hundred twenty pounds. He was dark skinned, balding, and seemed to have gone to seed. He had these large, wandering eyes that seemed to be roving like security cameras. He was the Israeli that I had mentioned earlier. But at this first encounter, all I knew was that he was in tight with the AQ boys.

We shared a bit of cautious, small talk, the kind prisoners who aren't sure of each other have. You have to do that so that you don't end up being friends with some child molester or rapist. But Jack was alright. He had been involved in the misappropriation of two million dollars worth of jewelry and diamonds from one of his businesses in the United States. He also had import/export business in Israel, Morocco, Spain, France, and Gibraltar.

Just for the record: import/export is synonymous with organized crime. The only things that really ever get exported are drugs, guns, and stolen things. Yeah, sometimes bananas or coffee surrounds them; but it's all just a game, and Jack was probably a player if the U.S. was trying to bring him back. I just filed away all of the interesting details and gave him the quick summary of my plight. (Bla, bla, bla, the U.S. stuck it to me.) He listened intently, nodding every so often as if he already knew my story – and not the line that I had put out to the gossipers.

As we were talking, some of the AQ boys started showing up and sitting at their usual table away from everyone else. Jack excused himself, and then went to the AQ boys and talked – in Arabic. A few seconds later they were nodding, and he turned and invited me to join them. And that is how the 'al Qaeda breakfast,' as U.S. Intelligence agents later called it, began.

If I could go back to that moment and decide again whether or not to enter their world, knowing what I do now about how it all turned out, and the terrible things that were confided to me, I'm not sure if I would. Once you open up a can of worms like that, you can never get the lid on again.

And there are things that I know, now, that I can never unlearn.

SIX: There is no James Bond here

I think that it might be interesting if you knew the system that we were using to transfer information from inside the Spanish Prison back to the United States, where people, who are much more intelligent and astute as to the value of such information, would be ready to analyze whatever fruit our operation would bear. I was certain that my information would make it to people who would interpret it in a timely manner, or turn it over to other people who could do so. I mean, surely after 9/11 we have worked out the kinks in our intelligence agencies' abilities to collate and share information in a way that would be useful to save lives. Well, the reality is – nothing has really changed. We just have more organizations to drop the ball. There are far too many nodes.

Our stealth system was called the Public telephone. Let me further explain. I would gather information in two-day bundles (48 hours worth of Intel) and transcribe as much as I could onto various legal documents and note paper, (papers and documents that I would later smuggle out of Spain). Then I would go to the common area in our unit where there were two telephones that could be used to make collect calls. That was where about thirty or forty of us would wait in line each day for our turn to use the phone. Now, if you didn't want to make collect calls, you could purchase calling card minutes from the Italians – that was their hustle.

So after I bought a couple of calling cards, I started making my information dumps. I would call my attorney on a non-secure, public phone line, and when he would answer, I would stand by for the barrage of questions. I tried to smile and laugh, to seem nonchalant, as I outlined to him what I had learned from my various sources and contacts within the al Qaeda cell into which I was slowly being immersed. I didn't want everyone to know that I was working as a spy for the US Government. Stuff like that gets you killed and not in a *fast, lights-out* kind of way. (It was more like a *we're going to start at your kneecaps and work our way up until you go into shock* kind of way.) So, I was just a certain degree of paranoid as I worked. They say that the best point-man is a paranoid schizophrenic. That's because he won't miss the wire.

I was always careful not to color my information with personal bias because that is one of the main reasons that HUMINT (human intelligence) can be flawed and unreliable. Very often, the spy sees what he wants to see, then the analysts see what they want to see, and some bombs get dropped 6,000 miles away. The job of a spy isn't to make judgments on what is or isn't important. The spy is no more than a human recording device.

He is to report as much as he can and let people with really high I.Q.'s and no social skills distill his Intel. I tried to relay the information that I thought was timely, first. I got almost everything written down so that when I went back to the US, I would be able to hand it over to my handler(s). I had twenty or thirty pages of hand written notes when it was all over.

As it turned out we, (my attorney and I), were working for several agencies. There was the Naval Investigative Service, the Central Intelligence Agency, the State Department, and possibly the Federal Bureau of Investigation. There may have been more of them, but I'm not certain who all of the players were. If all of this ever comes out in front of some senate hearing, then we'll probably learn who everyone was, and who to blame for the inaction. Most likely that will occur right before my car accident, or heart attack, or radiation overdose.

So, I'm making my information dumps over regular phone lines to my attorney. Often, when I would call, there were intelligence agents in the background asking me questions and telling me where to focus my antennae. I was directed several times in that manner, and my focus was redirected often. The funny thing about all this was that I kept expecting some kind of James Bond gadgetry. You know, some super sleuth micro telephone device – something cool? No. Apparently that kind of technology hasn't made it to the *War on Terror* yet.

Or, they thought that I was full of crap and didn't want to waste valuable taxpayers dollars on some ignorant pursuit. (Gosh. Iraq war, Afghanistan – I'm confused.) Well, I guess we can just pray that they'll get a sufficient budget, someday. We all have our fingers crossed.

I had friends in that prison that had cell phones smuggled in for less than 400 euros. At the very least, a secure cellular or satellite secure phone could have been provided. I couldn't understand why what we were doing was not considered important enough to warrant a better line of communication.

Later, I came to realize that it must have been for the sake of deniability. If they ever used funds to aid in my *work*, then there would be a paper trail that linked them directly to this dirty little Op. Then somebody would have to actually admit that they were working this gag, and answer a bunch of questions about how and why we probably let 191 people die in Madrid, Spain, when we had an American on the inside of the al Qaeda cell, that was an instrumental part of the plot. But let's not get ahead of ourselves.

I was doing this every couple of days, and even though we were taking huge risks, it was paying off a bit. As I will explain later, we hit on several good pieces of intelligence; and we did it in a timely enough manner that the US government could act on it. What they did was another matter altogether, but they did have the information. They seemed more interested in the financial side – the terrorists' funding – than in the terrorists themselves, locations of training camps, tactics, or terrorist plots! All of which I got for them. Yet all they ever acted on was the money. That's the part of all this that is really going to piss you off.

Welcome to the bureaucratic labyrinth that is "International Terrorism."

I believe that in some darker place, beyond our world, there are several hundred voices asking why their lives ended on March 13, 2004. They are calling out from one of those places that the living choose not to talk or even think about – that haunting place where whispers and screams are drowned and choked in the nothingness, and those cries that make it through the darkness are asking – what happened? Where did it all go?

And they are not sad when I hear them – they are angry.

SEVEN: You don't know Jack

I'll take you through the different players, now. As I quickly do, you'll start to see how complex it can get.

My first target was Jack. I refer to him as a target because it dehumanizes him; lessens the emotional toll that it might take on the vacuum that is my soul. At sniper school they have a famous question on one of the written tests where you have a target in your sights, and he holds up a small child in order to obstruct your shot at his upper lip.

The question is basically, "What do you feel?"

The correct answer is – *recoil.*

A target is an object, nothing more. Jack was an object that I had to understand, and though complex and intriguing, he was still just a thing.

Yaarok Asraf, known as Jack, was my first objective. He was the Israeli that I mentioned earlier, and I needed him to get in with the real bad guys. I first found it very odd that Jack was hanging around the AQ boys. As a general rule Muslims and Israelis don't get along so well. Jack's background was that his parents were a mixture of Israeli, Moroccan, and Lebanese. He was a dark-complexioned, slightly balding man with big liquid eyes set deep into his head. He was a bit overweight, but still active in his long *power walks.* He wore nice clothes, which included high-dollar jewelry and watch to match. There was plenty of *bling* for old Jack. He spoke several languages including Arabic, Hebrew, Spanish, and French. He seemed like a luxury car salesman, the kind of guy who'd be more than willing to help you part with two or three hundred thousand bucks.

I first thought that the AQ boys were just hanging around him because he had money. In a prison environment people will often flock around those with plenty of cash. Although, I guess they do that in any environment. As I got to know more about this curious alliance, I began to learn that the story was much darker. Jack had made most of his money doing import/ export, which we all know runs hand-in-hand with organized crime. He had offices in Morocco, Spain, France, Israel, Gibraltar, and some other more obscure locations.

He said that his main business was cheap clothing, but curiously, he was also involved in several jewelry stores. A jewelry store is not usually sinister, but some of Jack's business partners were involved in a rather large On-line gambling firm in Gibraltar. That firm was explained to me as a very large money laundering operation. His associates were also connected to Safra bank, and there were all kinds of seedy connections between the Russian Mob and various other groups using this bank to move nearly 100 million dollars in illicit funds.

So I was thinking that his angle was financial. Maybe he bankrolled Jihad. Who knew for sure what his religious beliefs really were. His parents were from both Jewish and Arab descent, and that could leave a brain pretty conflicted.

Jack explained to me that he was a former member of the Israeli Military, namely in a department called, Shin bet. That is essentially a military intelligence unit. I couldn't really tell what to believe, and what not to, so all I did was continue to note the major points and hope that it would all piece together. He also told me that he had made tons of cash by going in with contractors and rebuilding places that had been destroyed, places like Lebanon, Israel, New York. He said that after a storm, or a bombing, there was so much money being spent on reconstruction that a clever contractor could make more money than he could count.

That must be a bunch because most of the Jewish guys I know are very good at math. I then wondered if he just waited around until a bomb went off and then brought in his construction guys to cash-in.

As I got closer to him, we began to talk about both politics and religion, two subjects which I was still "undecided" on.

That's how it works. Spies don't need strong opinions. You can't be too outspoken or even too much of a supporter of the cause. They'll eventually see right through it. The target needs to believe that they are the ones converting you – showing you the path. A guy with heavy opinions might be spy, but a guy who's on the fence is a *prospect.* So I listened intently as Jack tried to convert me.

I remember when we were walking one morning, and he stopped and turned. Looking very intently at me he said, "You have some Jewish blood in your family?" It was as much a statement as it was a question – as if he somehow *knew*.

"Well, of course, Jack, However did you guess?" I told him that my grandparents on my father's side were Jewish. Who knows, maybe they were? Jack smiled self-assuredly and winked. He told me that he could tell when he first met me. I shrugged. A Jew knows a Jew, I suppose. Nothing gets past old Jack.

It seemed like after that epiphany, Jack just opened up to me. He told me about a jewelry scam for a couple million dollars out of New Jersey. He told me about brokering MANPADs (Man Portable Air Defense Systems) to different buyers in North America. It was basically a Stinger Missile sale.

You see, when the Russians invaded Afghanistan the United States was supporting the Mujahedeen. One of the ways in which they did this was to supply both funding and weapons to the Afghani fighters. At that time we were in the middle of the Cold war, trying to stop the menacing spread of Communism in its tracks. The US decided that part of its support would be to offer U.S. built Stinger Missiles at the price of US$ 50,000.00 a pop.

So the Mujahids conjured up enough cash and favor to purchase about 15,000 of them. That's what we call in the business, *a shitload* of surface-to-air missiles – the funny thing is that they are so easy to use that a sixth grader can fire one if he feels inclined.

Here are the stats on the Stinger missile:

- Length: 5 feet (1.5 meters)

- Diameter: 2.75 inches (7 cm)
- Weight: 22 pounds (10 kg)
- Weight with launcher: 34.5 pounds (15.2 kg)
- Explosives: 2.2 pounds, impact fuse (explodes on contact with target)
- Speed: 1,500 mph (2,400 kph, Mach 2)
- Altitude Range: Approximately 11,000 feet (3 km)
- Distance Range: Approximately 5 miles (8 km)

These missiles are almost idiot proof. They are so simple to use, in fact, that they ran the Russians right out of Afghanistan. Sounds like a happy ending? Here's the good news: No more invasion and only a couple thousand Stingers were used in the process. Bad news: The Mujahedeen fell in love with their toys and decided not to sell the remaining 10 or 12 thousand missiles back to the U.S. – even after being offered nearly twice the original price.

So all of these shoulder launched monsters disappeared – Poof! – and they were gone. They are now cached all over the Middle East, Northern Africa, and Europe. Some have even crossed the drink and made it to the Americas. They can easily catch a passenger plane on landing or takeoff; or a bus; or a train; or a – well, you get the point.

At any rate, Jack had claimed to have been involved in the black market sale of a couple of these death sticks. The more that I learned about him, the more I considered that it was possible that he was still working for the Israelis. He probably was not working in a military capacity, but maybe Mossad or some related unit. Perhaps he was doing exactly what I was doing. I couldn't verify any of his information, but then it didn't really matter.

He wasn't my major target, not exactly. But he was peripherally connected to the AQ boys, so he was important all the same. Also, there was the possibility that he was rogue, just working in between the lines. Some people start out with the best of intentions and end up losing their idealism and turning to capitalism. The difference between a good spy and a double agent is the bank account. People, no matter how noble and idealistic, will turn. Maybe its sex that lures them – maybe its cash, blackmail, extortion, disenfranchisement in the government, lost patriotism, or whatever. (What difference does it really make? Greed almost always wins in the end.)

Jack could be so many things, and I didn't know which. I started hearing things about the Dutch during conversations between Jack and the AQ boys. I heard Jack and the others mentioning Holland, and the Dutch, and all sorts of related things. I figured something might be up, so I reported it to my attorney during one of our information dumps.

In the background one of the guys asked about my source. I described Jack and gave his legal name, and then I waited with silence on the other end of the line.

I could hear muffled conversation and then one of the nameless voices told me to "stay away from Jack."

What?

I didn't understand.

It was explained to me that I was to give Jack plenty of room, and not to concentrate on his activities. It was *hands off* on Yaarok Asraf. So, at least now I had my suspicions confirmed. He was working for somebody. I didn't know who, but that wasn't really important to me. My job hadn't changed. Get close to the AQ boys. Jack was just a stepping-stone to bigger targets. (Just for the record, I still think he was dirty, even if he was a spook.)

Over the next several weeks I heard a lot of discussion about the Dutch. I continued to report this to my attorney and the faceless voices. I was reminded to back off of Jack. I started to wonder if I was just being paranoid and reading too much into nothing. (And really, what the hell do I know about being a spy?)

Almost exactly six weeks later a group claiming to be associated with, or part of, Al Qaeda bombed the Dutch Embassy in Riyadh. Kind of spooky, I thought. On the next call to my attorney I was told that everyone was now 'very interested' in what information I could provide. Then again, maybe I was just lucky.

I started to get this uneasy feeling that maybe I wasn't lucky.

My religion – of science and physics - doesn't have room for luck, only uncertainty. You see, it's different when you read about these guys in the newspaper, or on CNN. When you actually live with them and have a relationship with them, you start to see just a glimpse of just how cold and horrifying humans can be.

If they want to get you . . . you're dead.

EIGHT: Maybe he's onto something?

After the Dutch embassy-bombing in Riyadh, Saudi Arabia, people seemed to be much more interested in my Intel.

Now to be fair, one hit doesn't mean I was really on to anything. Just like gang members talk to their friends around the country, so do Muslim extremists, and my information was probably not accurate enough to have done much good. I suppose they could have put all of the Dutch embassies on *high-alert*, or beef up security around Dutch owned facilities. Heightened security measures might have helped save a few lives and help to minimize the property damage, but who can be certain?

What I needed to do was get accurate, verifiable Intel that could establish my contacts as being on the inside, in some way directly connected to the higher-ups at al Qaeda. I had to get close to the *Shot-callers.* I didn't only need this for the sake of establishing my credibility with the intelligence guys, but I had to have it for my own piece of mind. I needed proof that this was real, that this wasn't another Oklahoma City, where all sorts of suspects may or may not be legitimate. I wasn't fishing for scapegoats; I needed to hook the real thing. The only way that was going to happen was if I was much closer to the AQ boys. I needed to be in with them, not just a friend of Jack's. Fringe association was not going to be close enough.

As I was considering ways to achieve this goal, a little piece of fortuity fell in my lap. One of the AQ boys, a *mechanic* by the name of Mohammed (for obvious reasons I will leave out the last names), began speaking to me. He had homes or locations rather, in Spain and France. He was Algerian by birth, but like so many of his countrymen, he moved to France.

You see, France occupied Algeria for over a century until Charles De Gaulle ended the occupation in the sixties, withdrawing French forces and giving Algeria its autonomy. Incidentally, it nearly cost De Gaulle his life on several occasions as pissed-off military men from the French Foreign Legion and the French Army tried to have him assassinated. I experienced there, still, a general hatred for De Gaulle in the Legion. Anyway, there are plenty of Algerians in France, and this particular AQ boy wanted me to teach him English. (Oh, those inscrutable al Qaeda operatives – always looking to better themselves through education.)

I recognized that this was a good opportunity. If I got in with Mohammed, then I would be inside their barrier. This was a feat because there were several attempts to pierce the invisible wall that the AQ boys had around them by other intelligence agents. I am almost certain that at least one French, and several Spanish agents, tried to ingratiate themselves with the AQ boys, but to no avail. Strangely enough, one of them disappeared, (but who knows?)

The Spanish authorities at the behest of the U.S. Government were holding Mohammed. He, along with about 13 or 14 other terrorist suspects, was waiting patiently in Valdemoro prison (a.k.a. *Terrorist University*) while the Spanish government tried to figure out how to keep them illegally imprisoned without having other terrorists blow stuff up all over the country.

The Spanish were already having their own problems with local terrorists, namely E.T.A (Basque Separatists). The last thing that they needed was al Qaeda feeling like they should influence world politics by making things like trains and buses detonate. That's a literary device known as *foreshadowing.* So, while the Spanish Ministry of the Interior was juggling the legal and moral ramifications of holding a bunch of legal *residents* without charges, they were also being pressed into sending troops into Iraq to support the U.S. led War of Terror, I mean *War on Terror.* (my mistake – quite a juggling act, indeed.)

From the way that the other people, guards included, treated the AQ boys, I'd say they were clearly apprehensive. They were given plenty of space, and nobody pressed them for anything. (Funny, how nobody ever tries to shake down a Muslim extremist for his lunch money.) It was not lost on me the realization that if they found out what I was doing, they would probably not want me to continue breathing. They have a penchant for large knives, those extremists. So, I settled myself each day to walk and talk with Jack and the AQ boys, to teach Mohammed English, and to not get killed.

My buddy Mohammed's background was that he had a family in France, and that he worked as a mechanic. His family had left Algeria sometime in the late '80s. He was very crafty, and seemed to pick things up very quickly. I figured him for a bomb technician or weapons fabricator. He was about 5'5" with a thin frame and rather frail features. His head was shaven, as are most of the active Cell members for al Qaeda.

Those guys that you see on television with all their scraggly beards, like Osama Bin Laden, are not actual operators. That long beard that will land you spread-eagle on the floor of an airport is more or less a status symbol for a religious leader such as an Imam. The soldiers themselves are clean-shaven and businesslike. They have no facial hair of any kind. They even pluck their armpits in some cases, depending on their particular religious beliefs. I found that to be a little anal, but I digress. Mohammed had small intelligent eyes that were greenish and curious as they moved back and forth. He was very polite and spoke a little English. When I watched him look at things, it was as if he was a architect or a scientist. He kind of took things in dimensionally.

He explained to me, after a few English lessons, that he wanted to sound like a Canadian or at least an experienced traveler. He said that they had people in Quebec, Canada, and that he could go there without too many problems. I was fairly certain that he was an operator relatively low on the al Qaeda totem pole. I imagine that we'll find his DNA on some large-scale explosive device sometime in the future. He was just one of those hands-on, clever kinds of guys, the nice man down the hall who can fix anything, a very polite, capable terrorist. He was a devout Sunni Muslim, and there was no doubting that he would do whatever was asked of him. He was calm, quiet, and methodical, and that pretty much equals dangerous. There was something else about him that stuck out in my mind: he was already dead. What I mean is that he was cold and resolved in his actions. He accepted, probably long ago, that he would die for his faith. The Samurai say that one must live in this manner, as though he were already dead, in order to excel in your calling as a warrior. Mohammed had died, in his mind, long ago.

The issue was foreclosed.

He was without fear – a walking ghost.

We began studying together after the morning *Al Qaeda breakfast.* We'd usually work for about 30 or 45 minutes until the questions started. He wanted to know where I grew up, and what I studied in school. It almost goes without saying that a good person goes to *university.* Life is the continuous pursuit of education. Almost every terrorist I ever met had a college degree or five. He was interested in what I thought about my time in the Navy, my experiences in the French Foreign Legion, and about my political views. I always stayed right in the middle of the road with my answers. He asked me about religion. I explained to him that I was undecided, but that I was open to anything that *felt* right.

He wanted to know about my favorite music, my favorite football team, and my favorite ice cream. At first glance, one might think that he was asking all of these questions because he wanted to be my friend, or because he was fascinated in the American way of life, like so many other non-Americans. But none of that mattered to him. He was checking me out. He was determining if I was somebody he could trust, or a spy - who would have to be killed in a very public way so as to send a warning out to others. Trust me or kill me, that was it. Try walking that tightrope.

So I told him the truth, or enough of it so that when they checked out my story they would not have to fillet me later. An angry American mercenary on the run from the law was the angle I played. And really, I didn't mind the Q and A sessions. It was just like a job interview; accept that instead of working for a company with a 401K, I was applying to a firm with AK47's and C-4. Jihad is the new Microsoft. The good news was that they hired from within! I answered him directly, joking every now and again, keeping it light. I maintained good eye contact, no shifty eye movements, limited physical gesturing, hands folded in front of me. There were none of the obvious deceptive signs.

A couple weeks of this went by and then the questions changed in their tone. Something else happened, too: another one of the AQ boys started to join us for our question time. We'll call him Nebar. Once he started showing up the questions took on a more tactical angle. They wanted to know about my experience with small arms (pistols, small machine guns), and about hand-to-hand combat. When the questions got to be military oriented, (my experience in the US Navy, and French Foreign Legion), Nebar seemed to be the one leading the questions. When the questions were technical, it was Mohammed who did the asking. When I answered, they would look at each other briefly and then turn back to me. Pretty soon we were having group discussions with all five of the AQ boys. Oddly, Jack was not invited, or perhaps he had been uninvited. I'm not sure, and I didn't ask. Whatever the case was, we were now having discussions on all sorts of things from business to science, military strategy to comedy. It became an open dialogue.

I thought that I was finally making it in. My Russian and English buddies told me to be careful not to get labeled as a terrorist by the Screws – prison term for guards, or functionarios. I told them that I was just having fun, pretending that I was a *real* bad guy. But if I was to tell you the truth, I wanted the AQ boys to take me in. I needed to become one of these guys. That was the only way that I was ever going to get close to anybody and anything valuable.

If you want to understand a terrorist, much less catch one . . . you must become one. I had the resume; I just hadn't finished the interviews, yet. But each day I was getting closer. Each call I made to my attorney was more detailed. I was closing in on something. I just didn't know what.

And then the screws told me to pack my stuff.

NINE: Being transferred!

We had just gotten through collecting some money and a television from a guy who had a bit of an outstanding debt. I was acting as a translator on this particular deal.

The Russians, when they get angry, seem to lose their ability to properly enunciate in Spanish, and though I only spoke a bit of the native tongue, it was better than an irate psychopath from St. Petersburg. I helped mediate the collection negotiations, and my English friend James helped fill in the gaps here and there. We all made a good team. Basically, if we came knocking on your door, you did something to get us there. When we showed up, there wasn't any talk about *if* there was a debt, only how much was owed, and how it would be satisfied. It hardly ever got really violent. But then, I'm probably not the right person to judge what the baseline for violence is.

So now we're coming back down after our little negotiation, making sure that not too many people saw what happened, and I hear my name being butchered over the intercom. James and I look at each other quizzically, and then hear my name again. The first thing that popped into our heads was that there was some problem with my last cellmate. He was a Columbian guy who liked to smoke in the room. I had made it clear, in a rather non-verbal way that he was not to be living in that cell by the end of the day.

"Fucking grass!" James said, an affectionate term the English use for a snitch or a rat, as in *Snake in the grass*.

I nodded. Most likely he had grassed me up to the guards while we were sorting out this other debt related matter upstairs.

He and I finished our business with our Russian partners and then headed to the center of the unit where we would talk to the screws (guards) through a couple of inches of Plexiglas. As we approached, one of the screws waved me toward a small panel that they could slide open to hand people their mail.

"Tu vas a ir a Modulo cuatro," he said. You're going to go to Modulo (unit) four.

That's the high-crimes/special management unit. That's where they put the dangerous guys: the killers, the psychopaths, and the terrorists. All the best parts of the prison environment are all together in one unit that is locked down almost all the time. No fun. No freedom. No more al Qaeda breakfasts.

James started to argue in Spanish, but the guard just held up a sheet of paper with some red stamps on it and some unintelligible Spanish bureaucratic babble.

"You're fucking dangerous, Jay," James said with an odd glare. I shrugged. He sure knows how to make a guy feel special.

I figured that my background in the military, or as a professional fighter might have finally made its way to people in the prison who didn't want me to 'freak-out' or cause more trouble, or maybe my Columbian cellmate had grassed me up.

Whatever the case was, I had 20 minutes to gather up all of my personal belongings and be ready to transfer.

As we turned, Jack was there asking what was going on. He then approached the screws and asked them the reason for my transfer, but the guard just gave up and walked away shaking his head in frustration. Jack wanted me to fight this thing. What thing? There was nothing to fight. I was on my way to Modulo 4. I was now considered a dangerous inmate, and would be treated as such.

I went to my room and gathered my stuff: a large camouflage bag with all of my clothes and various notes and court papers. I headed back down and shook hands with all of the Russians. Then James and I shook hands, and he gave me some contact numbers. Jack was there too, and in his outstretched hand was some cash. I didn't feel right taking it, but I accepted the money anyway. Then the AQ boys came down. They gathered around me and took their turns thanking me for all of the help. Mohammed then pulled me aside and Nebar joined him. In a hushed voice he said, "When you get where you're going, find Nader." There was a palpable amount of reverence as they said his name. They continued, "Tell him that you are a friend of ours." And with that ,they nodded, shook my hand, and quickly scampered away.

Three things popped into my mind as possible explanations for my relocation. One: I'm just a really dangerous guy, and the Spanish didn't want me in the population with non-violent people like, for example, that little Columbian grass that was being relocated from my cell – maybe.

Two: The U.S. intelligence guys had somehow gotten me switched to a unit to get closer to somebody higher up on the hierarchical ladder within al Qaeda. It was a possibility.

And three: Somehow Mohammed and Nebar had affected my relocation to get me closer to somebody named Nader. I didn't know which was more likely. Even as I write this, there is compelling information to support all three theories. Whatever the case, I was now going to be in a whole new world. At that moment, I realized with total clarity, that this was for real. If I messed up now – well, you know the deal.

One of the screws started slapping the Plexiglas and pointed to a large cage door that I was to wait by. I nodded to everybody and then headed off toward the gate. Another gate ground to a close behind me, leaving me alone in this large, square room of green concrete and just the slightest smell of musty coffee sewn in on some molecular level. Everything got quiet. A few seconds later the entire panel in front of me started to move to the left. As it disappeared into a recess in the wall, I was motioned again to head out.

Like a rat in a maze, I was moved from one room to the next, then down a hall, then two more green rooms. Five minutes later I was being strip-searched for weapons.

Welcome to Modulo 4.

"Watch what you say in here," one of the screws said in Spanish. "The people here can become violent and hurt you. Even kill you."

That's a sword that cuts both ways.

TEN: High Crimes Unit

The welcoming that I received in the High Crimes/High Security unit was less than warm. They call it "Preventivo" in Spanish, but we call it "Modulo 4." It's the last place that you end up in Valdemoro prison.

In this unit, as it was explained to me, we were always being watched – studied. We were only out of our cells for 2 to 3 hours a day, and that was if we were on our best behavior. Our meals were served through a small hole in the door with a sliding metal panel. The cells were located on the second and third floors of the unit. All of the cells were single-man and stale. Picture something out of a cheap European film and you're getting close.

The floors were painted green. The toilets were part of those sink-toilet combos made of stainless steel by some large factory in North Korea. The heating was handled through the floor – when it was cold out, the floor heated up – nifty. Each room had three, thin rectangular window panels that could be opened to reveal the *yard* below. The windows were only about 4 inches wide, so there was no danger of you slipping out into the night, not that there was anywhere to go if you did.

The yard was even better. In the hour or two that you were allowed to visit: you would be surrounded by a thick concrete wall that went about 24 feet into the air. Above the edge of the wall were several rows of stretched concertina wire sharp enough that flies and birds didn't dare land on its razor edges. It frequently made Swiss cheese out of the soccer balls that were unlucky enough to make their way that high. Not that there were ever enough people for a soccer game anyway; only half of the 40-man unit was allowed out at the same time.

Lonely doesn't quite describe it. Of the twenty people in my group, only about five or six of them were physically able to play any kind of sports. Several of them were never allowed out of their cells.

About half of them were on a perpetual Thorazine or Methadone shuffle. That's where the drugged-out recipient of said pharmaceutical, shuffles his feet back and forth all day long between dosages of his drug. Sometimes these zombies will slide along until their shoe soles are completely worn through and their feet are leaving bloody skid marks on the concrete. Basically, these junkies are just walking themselves to death. Remember, this isn't an American prison. Things work differently. You're alone here.

Of those who were not medicated, the rest were a whole different kind of dangerous. In my group were 4 ETA (Basque Separatists), 2 Israeli Ecstasy traffickers, 2 Italian drug/cigarette traffickers, 2 Mercenaries, 1 Moroccan hit man, 1 French Crime boss, and 3 al Qaeda detainees that included a certain high-ranking Imam named: Nader.

Oh yeah, and me.

During the first week I was confined to my cell. I guess that they do this to calm the new guys down, make them appreciate any privileges that might be given to them at a later time.

Once that week was up, I was allowed to leave my cell once a day. Each day the *recreational* time would alternate from morning to afternoon. During that time you were allowed to communicate with the other few inmates; grab a cup of coffee or a snack from a tiny commissary cart that would appear behind a barred window for a couple of minutes each day; work-out in the tiny little square of a rec yard; or take a shower. My routine was to get my cell cleaned as quickly as possible and then head down to the yard. From there I would do calisthenics for about an hour and then head to the showers. I made this my *system* until I learned who everyone was.

I didn't want to immediately introduce myself to Nader for several reasons. First, I wasn't sure who he was, and I didn't want to seem like a spook asking around for an al Qaeda shot-caller. They had probably been dealing with intelligence agents for some time now, and were getting quite adept at sniffing them out. Second, I was trying not to get killed by any of the other dangerous people that I was now living among. My little hunt for al Qaeda was only one part of the equation. I also needed to know who everyone else was; know my enemies and my allies. You must understand your culture and the rules of your society, no matter how large or small it may be. I kept quiet until I had the lay of the land.

The first guy that I met was Pasquale, an Italian mercenary who had started his criminal career as a Fascist Terrorist with the Italian Red Brigade. After a few trashcan bombs and a few shootouts with the police, he had to leave Italy. He decided to hook up with some Americans who were planning a coup attempt in the South American country of Chile. Some guy named Allende was running for President and the U. S. thought it better if their guy Pinochet would be in power. The *company* had tried to rig the election, but you know how democracy can sometimes be? You give the people a chance and they'll bite you in the ass. The people spoke loud enough that the CIA couldn't get Pinochet elected. So the fallback plan was an overthrow, a rather common motif for the U.S. when dealing with South and Central American politics. Anyway, Pasquale joined that little gig, and then headed back across the drink and ended up making his way into Lebanon. He was the chief of security for the Armenian Christians' sector in Beirut. This was in the early eighties when the city was being constantly shelled by the *USS New Jersey* – parked a couple of miles offshore.

From there he spent some time as a Colonel with the Croatian Army doing ethnic *cleansing* and that kind of thing. Then he turned to swat-style bank robberies and extortion. Anyway, he had an exciting life full of twists and turns, and along the way he stopped off in Spain where he was grabbed by an INTERPOL team that had accidentally gotten a hold of him while looking for some other people. So: naturally, he and I hit it off.

Pasquale and I started working out on the yard, stretching, shadowboxing, and shooting the basketball – things to keep us occupied. It was nice to be around a guy who shared similar interests such as warfare for the sake of the fight, no political or religious undertones, loving the bullet because it is pure and simple, and never deceives you. Once he and I had gotten used to each other, he started giving me the run down on who the other prisoners were. He carried himself like a seasoned pro.

As it turned out, this unit – Modulo 4 – was almost exclusively for people who were wanted in other countries; Extradition cases like me. Some of them, like the al Qaeda guys, were claiming *Hazard Politic* status (political Refugee), and were trying to fight their extraditions. Others, like the Israelis and the Italians, were just trying to go to the country with the cleanest prisons and the nicest food service. None of them would probably ever see the outside of a prison unless they could buy their way out of trouble. Though, that was not entirely impossible, because they were all remarkably well connected.

After a week or two, I was introduced to Farid. He was a French crime boss who had property and businesses all over Spain and France. He was wanted for the conspiracy to murder about 20 or 30 competitors in France. Farid was Algerian/French, whose family had started several restaurants in Marseilles and Aubagne. He was heavily into Arms and Drug Trafficking. He assured me that basically, he was a nice guy. He made it clear that everyone that he ordered killed had it coming.

Under that rather loose definition I suppose that we all have it coming.

He was quite certain that upon his return to France that he would beat the charges because nobody would ever testify against him. People don't talk about "Fa-fa." Farid was a really likable guy. He was about 5' 10", dark complexioned with black curly hair. He was educated and a very inspiring person to talk to. Full of energy and very self-confident, everything he spoke about was with spirit and enthusiasm. Nothing was boring to him. Nothing was unimportant. He seemed to find a lesson in everything. He started to join us, and we would discuss current events and *real politics.*

You can learn a lot about a person from their take on politics, even the subtle and slight changes in gesture and attitude when discussing seemingly unimportant issues. Psychology is all about nuance.

Once I had met and established rapport with Farid, he began to introduce me to the others. I met the Israelis, the other Italians, and then . . . the ranking al Qaeda detainees.

It was after one of our morning workouts. Pasquale, Farid, and I had been working out while three of the al Qaeda detainees walked back and forth in the small yard, as they usually did. They rarely associated with anyone else, and when they did, they were only exchanging pleasantries. I remember it being cool out and cloudy to the point of almost being dark. A storm was threatening to rip the air apart and unload whatever seawater it had taken hostage.

We were cooling down, stretching our legs after the workout when the al Qaeda guys made their way over to us. There were two bigger guys who acted like minders (bodyguards), and a smaller man with the telltale Osama beard behind them. They approached slowly with the disquieting rumble of thunder in the background. None of us said much as they approached. The two front men shook all of our hands, said something to Farid in Arabic, and then turned toward me. They shook my hand in turn and then slowly, sternly, the third man approached. If I were to give you my first impression it would be, *textbook Muslim terrorist*. He had the beard, the piercing eyes, and something else that I can't put into words.

But, I suppose, the first thing that comes to mind is *driven*. He was intent and decisive. I felt like I was supposed to bow or something by the way that everyone revered him. He slowly outstretched his hand and I did the same. Both of his hands clasped mine as more thunder growled around us. The wind started to pick up as dust and paper began to dance around us to invisible music.

"My name is Nader," he said very clearly in Algerian-accented English. "I have heard some things about you."

ELEVEN: What *real* Bad guys look like

I spent the rest of that day in my cell while the windows were being pounded by rain as heavy as rocks. Under the curtain of all of that noise, I was left alone with my thoughts. Because of the new situation of me being in this unit, I would only be making my information dumps twice a week.

That was probably best anyway because the less times I was seen using the phone, the better. This unit was so quiet that it wouldn't be much of a trick to listen while somebody was using the one phone they had available. We weren't even allowed to dial the number ourselves; it had to be handled by the screws so that they could log our calls. Somewhere that logbook still exists.

What I thought most about was my new target, Nader. He had a dark complexion, was about 5'6", and maybe 140 pounds. His hair was starting to grey, and he looked weathered like an old sailor. He had two darkened marks above his eyebrows that had calcified from years of salat (prayer). Note: When anyone prays so much that they have permanent markings on their forehead, don't let them board the plane, or at least, make them check their baggage on an alternate flight. Anyway, Nader appeared to be the real deal. I knew that my infiltration needed to be perfect. I didn't have any room for error. He had asked me to walk with him the next time that we came down for rec, and I wanted to have myself prepared. As it turned out, chance prepared me.

I had been reading a book that had been loaned to me. It was about Carlos the Jackal and the Palestinian conflict with Israel. I chose it because I had read several Robert Ludlum books and in the Borne series, one of the main bad guys is Carlos the Jackal. I figured it would be neat to know the real story about this infamous terrorist. By chance, I had this book with me the next morning when I went downstairs for rec. I said hello to the gang of social deviants and made my way out to the still damp concrete. I set the book down beside my shirt and started the workout with my calisthenics routine. I was alone that morning because Pasquale was feeling a little sick from something that he had eaten the night before. "I am toilet today," were his exact words. We were served a lot of seafood and it didn't always sit too well with everyone.

As I was nearing the end of my workout, I noticed that Nader had come out with his goons and begun his walking. I could feel them watching me, the same intuitive way that you can kind of feel somebody *watching* you in an alley. You don't exactly know who or where, but you're sure that somebody is focused on you. You just hope that it's not through the scope of somebody's .308 sniper rifle.

I finished my routine and began to stretch – a little five-minute deal that keeps me from getting too sore. The goons headed inside the unit and I was left alone in the yard with

Nader. He walked toward me and nodded very graciously. He then looked down at the book about the Jackal.

"I know him," he said as he eyed the book.

I looked at the book and then back to Nader. "You know the writer?" I asked.

Nader smiled, "No, not the writer. I know Carlos."

"The Jackal. You know him?" I was a bit skeptical, because the book was only about six or seven years old and as of that printing Illich Ramirez Sanchez (a. k. a. Carlos the Jackal) was still at large, being hunted by several countries for "Terrorists activities" all over Europe and North Africa.

I knew from Farid and Pasquale that this man was an Imam (Muslim priest). I also knew from television that he was an al Qaeda suspect. You see, Pasquale and I had seen a news program on Spanish Television that showed the al Qaeda pyramid – the operational chart of all the important bad guys. Picture the food, but instead of protein and carbohydrates you have terrorists and insurgents.

I think that it was all propaganda, part of the build up for the War in Iraq. At the top of the pyramid were two people. Of course, Osama Bin Laden was one of them, and the second was none other than . . . Nader.

Yeah, that was one of those *Holy Shit* moments, pay dirt in the spy game. So I was well aware of who he was, or at least, who the Spanish media thought he was.

"Mr. Sanchez is a good Muslim now. He is in France, in prison. He and I were cellmates," Nader explained. Oh, gosh. He then enlightened me as to how the French made a deal with the Sudanese government for Carlos. The French agreed to stop arming the Rwandans who were fighting the Ugandans in North Central Africa. They had been selling some of the weapons to a Colonel Gurang who was in turn using those weapons in a civil war against the Sudanese government. Sudanese Intelligence then tricked Carlos and his family onto a plane and French Intelligence agents took him down. That occurred in 1997. Oh, and right after the French got Carlos, they began shipping the weapons again. Those pesky French! He had more details, but I think you get the point.

Nader was stranger than I had expected. He was more real, more human. To be honest, I'm not exactly sure what I expected him to be like. I wasn't sure if he would be the fire and lightning kind of extremist that I've grown accustomed to seeing on Al Jazeera or the soft-spoken warrior-poet type. Nader was something different.

First, he was very intelligent. He fluently spoke English, Arabic, Spanish, and French. He even spoke a little Russian. He was not a demanding man, but he was very confident, sure of his convictions. Most times he was reserved and contemplative. Then he would become animated all of the sudden while talking; then explain his point of view so clearly that you had no choice but to see his side of the issue, even if you didn't necessarily agree.

We walked that morning, talking about my time in France.

Oddly, he was much more interested in my experiences in the Legion, than in my life in America – although, that might have just been his way of gaining my confidence – the art of indirect advance. He and I were both working each other. I had decided early on to let Nader dictate where the conversations went. The one who has the ability to knowingly relinquish control of the personal dynamic to the other person is actually the one who is *in* control. Relationships are all a matter of bartering control. I, as an insignificant American gun-for-hire, was not going to be dictating the pace of anything when dealing with a top-ranking member of al Qaeda.

"I am Imam," he told me as we walked. "It is like a priest, but also very different. What do you know about the Muslim faith?"

I shrugged. "To be honest, I haven't really given religion much thought."

"I don't understand," he said, and he stopped walking and turned toward me. His eyes were wide and interested, searching for signs of something inside me.

I explained to him that I hadn't found a religion that fit in well enough with the world around us – a world with science, life, pain, chaos, suffering, love, racism, fear, marriage, sex, torture, disease, and tsunamis that kill 300,000 people in a day and all of it without explanation or reason. I shrugged to him. "I just don't really have an opinion on that stuff. The world seems too ugly."

He didn't argue with me, or try to change my mind. He just nodded, patted me on the shoulder, and we began walking again. We didn't speak about anything in particular. He talked a bit about life in Algeria. He had been an Algerian Military Officer. Later on I would come to learn that he had been forced to flee Algeria for his connection to a group called MAOL (*Movement Army Officers Libre*). This secret group of Algerian soldiers was all Muslim, and dedicated to keep Algeria from collapsing into civil war, or being ruled by corruption – which it was.

If you follow the history of Algeria you will note that the last several Presidents ended their rule by being assassinated. There are several factions at work in the country: Their secret service, the Algerian Military, the Algerian Police; and a group called unit 192, named for the January 1992 coup attempt and murder of several high-ranking military and political officials. The tentacles of each group seem to intertwine with the others, and there is a great deal of internal uncertainty which leads to violence most of the time. It's quite confusing.

He told me how he was notified that *they* were coming to arrest and kill him for his involvement in MAOL. As a military investigator, he was privy to a great deal of classified and sensitive material, and there was no way they would allow him to live. So he fled. He left his wife and children, his friends and family – everything.

He made it clear to me that he understood leaving your home country when it had turned against you. He knew about saying goodbye to your friends and family forever. He could relate to both loving and hating the same place for different reasons.

He then asked if I had ever read the Qur'an. I shook my head no. He told me that after contacting the *brothers*, that he would provide me a Qur'an in English. He also assured me that he wasn't trying to pressure me into making a decision or even to read it. But, if I chose to read it, then he would discuss the stories with me each day while we walked. I accepted his offer.

The next day we had our rec time in the afternoon. As Nader descended the stairs, he had a leather-bound Qur'an in his hands. Geez, this guy moves fast. He waited until we were outside and walking alone before he handed me the book. When he did, he studied my reaction.

"It must have been a lot of trouble to get this," I said. He just smiled. "English on one side, and Arabic on the other – however, our books start on the right, and our first page is in the position of the ending of Western books." He was telling me that the book was backwards or more likely, that we westerners were the backwards ones. I would probably agree to both.

And so, after a few minutes walking quietly beside him I said, "Tell me about Jihad."

He didn't seem surprised, or react in any perceivable way. He nodded slightly and then took my arm in his, as so many Arab men do as a show of friendship and respect.

"You tell me what you know of Jihad, and I will answer your questions." Al Qaeda wanted my opinion on the *service of god,* the highest service under Allah, Holy war.

All I could think about were those grainy images that had flashed by time and time again on CNN and MSNBC, images and pictures of torn and smoking buildings with blood and concrete, and metal rebar splayed in every direction; visions of people wearing sheets and blankets who couldn't do anything but wander aimlessly in the streets trying to find people that no longer existed. But the truth is, I was a dumb westerner. I was uneducated in the Muslim life and customs.

I didn't understand terrorism. As an American, I was too arrogant to ever ask the kind of questions that we should have all been asking ourselves. Not that I was mature enough to have understood, but then, Nader knew all of this the first time he had looked at me.

Some things you can't hide.

Some people see in you those missing parts that you might not even know are gone. He also saw something in me that he thought was worth the investment. Pasquale told me that he had never befriended somebody like he had me, and especially an American. He had plans. So did I.

My first class at Terrorist University was about to begin. It would be the scariest class that I would ever take.

TWELVE: Terrorism 101

I need to preface the information that follows. Over the course of my various conversations and dialogue with Nader, I learned a great deal of information.

However, if I were to give you a day-by-day, diary-like account, it would become very confusing because there was no set pattern for our discussions. You see, we didn't necessarily carryover our conversations from one day to the next. They kind of just happened.

In other words, one day we talked about several subjects and the next day we might or might not talk about the same things. But over time, the bulk of my knowledge and understanding evolved to a point where things started to become less convoluted. They coalesced into a much clearer picture as the details grew. Everything started to make more sense. I'm not sure if the analysts felt the same way, but it made enough sense to me. I will do my best to give you the most non-biased interpretation of what we spoke about.

Try to imagine, if you will, signing up for a Modern Art class. Nobody that you know has ever taken the class. They might have purchased books on tape, but not the real thing. On the first day you walk in and there is nobody else in the class. It's just you and the professor. As a matter of fact, his desk is right in front of yours – the whole auditorium for just you and the instructor. In he walks and you realize that it is Pablo Picasso. He explains that he will be teaching you modern art, and that his roommate used to be Leonardo De Vinci.

You need to understand that Nader was not just a terrorist, nor freedom fighter, extremist, or militant. He was one of the top 2 or 3 spiritual leaders for what we refer to as al Qaeda. If there was an academy awards show for influential bad guys then Nader and Osama would be walking down the red carpet while flash bulbs and microphones swarmed them like starving mosquitoes. They are at the top of their game.

One morning Nader and I were watching a television set in the day room. The news anchor was telling everyone that the US Military claimed Osama Bin Laden to be dead, that he was no longer among the living. Nader laughed to himself and threw up a dismissive hand, waiving the television off as we headed out to the rec (recreation) yard.

"You don't think that he's dead?" I asked.

"He is alive and well. He is in the *Tora Bora* Mountain range," he scoffed. "I could show you on a map," he added as his voice trailed off.

I later learned that Bin Laden was considered to be a great champion of the Muslim cause, but not much of a soldier or operator. Bin Laden comes from a very wealthy family, with roots in Yemen and Saudi Arabia.

Later, he did in fact show me on a map of Afghanistan. That's when he told me about Gulbuddin Hekmatyar. He came up during several different discussions. This man, Hekmatyar, is a warlord in Afghanistan who owns a great deal of property and businesses in and around Pakistan. Basically, Hekmatyar was supporting the Jihad effort by keeping supplies and money flowing right under the noses of U. S. and Afghani forces, and into the hands of the Mujahedeen. Many of them were hiding in and around the Tora Bora Mountain range, in a labyrinth of caves and hidden passages. Interestingly enough, a great deal of those caves and passages were built and or financed by the CIA in the '80s when the U.S. was supporting the Mujahedeen against the Soviets. Ahh, the Cold War. Don't you miss all those good times?

It was explained to me that Hekmatyar was bouncing back and forth across the Pakistan-Afghanistan border, paying-off anyone that asked questions. Don't let the rags fool you; the Mujahedeen are not hurting financially. There are plenty of prominent families and businessmen who support their cause. Hekmatyar had all kinds of strategies in place to move cash and enable travel for the Mujahedeen. He owned buses, taxis, boats, rental car agencies, hotels, restaurants etc. I was told that he owned over 10,000 vehicles between both countries.

Now, I can't verify all that, but apparently the U.S. Government and several news agencies agree because there have been several articles about a dangerous warlord named, 'Hekmatyar'.

There is an April 15, 2004, article in the Wall Street Journal that reported a Top Lieutenant, of a Warlord named,

"Hekmatyar" was arrested in Afghanistan by Peacekeepers. The man confirmed that Hekmatyar was indeed a warlord allied with the Taliban and al Qaeda. He may also have had ties to the Alkifah Refugee center in New York, which I will address in detail later.

In later conversations Nader was quite intent that I would meet Hekmatyar, because he was a very influential and important part of their cause. Our meeting would have probably been during the 2004 Hajj, which, incidentally, ended just days before the Madrid Train bombings on March 11th of that year. Many meetings occur over the course of the pilgrimage. It can turn into an extremist melting pot for al Qaeda members. And that's something else which I need to explain – the al Qaeda you think you know, and the real al Qaeda are two different things.

Television and politics have created this image of a giant evil menace as al Qaeda. In reality, that name translates to "the Base." The word Taliban means *Student.* There are many different groups that the media all lump under the umbrella of al Qaeda, but in reality each of the different organizations have different agendas. It is crucial to the process of mediation and peace that people start paying attention to which group takes credit for an attack or threat. Under careful scrutiny, you will see that many of the *terrorist attacks* that are quickly labeled al Qaeda, are in fact not so similar. There are different goals, different theologies, different targets, and different reasons. Al Qaeda is a stamp placed on everything that blows up because it seems to be a good way to rally support for the *War on Terror*. I'm not making a political statement one way or another; I just thought that it was important to know what you're being fed.

One afternoon, I was shown a picture of the Mecca in Saudi Arabia during the Hajj (the Muslim pilgrimage that every Muslim must go on if he can possibly afford it, at least once in his lifetime). In that picture there were so many people that they just looked like those grainy little dots that cover your television screen when your satellite cable is disconnected, but all of that static was human.

"One and one-half million people," Nader said. "They are all listening to an Imam."

"I bet it was hard to hear him," I noted. I'm so perceptive.

"You could hear every word that was said." Then he pointed to one of the little specs on the photograph. "That is me, a few years ago."

I squinted as I studied the photograph. "Geez – that's a lot of people." So many people in one place – all of them willing to sacrifice anything for what they believed in, and I'm not just talking about blowing themselves up.

No, religion in all forms has such a power over people that it cannot be denied as the greatest of all political and social motivators to impact humanity since we left the caves. There doesn't seem to be any greater power than faith. That rather frightening truth is probably one of the reasons I was so undecided about religion. So many lives silenced over differing theologies. It's really a turn-off for me, but then, this whole thing isn't about me. I'm insignificant. Nader was influential. He was both a religious and political force to be reckoned with. I can't recall the last time I spoke to 1.5 million people at a live venue, all of them hanging on my every word, looking for guidance, willing to act on whatever was asked of them no matter the personal cost. That's a lot of power.

Nader explained to me that people often know the right *path,* but that they must sometimes be pushed to make the first step of that journey. To him, any religion – not just the Muslim faith – was a long, winding trail that has all kinds of dead-ends and pitfalls with turns in every direction. There are tests, hurdles, and struggles just for the sake of suffering. In the end, faith had to carry you across the ravine.

He created for me an image of the end times. It was a rather grim picture of all the souls that lacked faith stuck below this narrow bridge. Around them were fire and disease, pain and chaos, and among these non-believers were knives, swords, blood, teeth and screaming – a rather horrifying image of the last remnants of humanity decaying into death, the people ripping each other apart. Above them on that narrow crumbling bridge were the believers. Their tests were also not completed, but they were as close as one can be to Allah.

"Allah is God," Nader said. "They are the same."

He assured me that there would be a final measurement of the way in which you had lived your life. Only then would one be granted access to that next place.

When I asked him what it would be like he answered, "Imagine passing a camel through the eye of a needle."

"What does that mean?" I asked, rather confused. He just smiled. I wanted him to think that things needed to be explained to me. As an intelligence source, it would help me immensely in the future – patterns in dialogue, that kind of thing.

When I asked about that place – Heaven – he said that it was something that no human could explain. To try to do so would be to attempt to know the mind of Allah, and that is something that no Imam would ever be able to do.

"You won't find faith," he would say, " . . . you will find belief."

I guess the rest would just take care of itself.

On occasion he would talk in these kinds of ambiguities, nearly riddles. I guess all religious types do that from time to time. Nader was perfectly coherent most of the time.

He and I began to discuss the Surah (chapters) that I had read in the Quran. I tried to read one each evening so that it would lead into our discussions. My thought process was: Start talking about the Quran, and surely some fire and lightening will come out. Then I could subtly edge the conversations into more violent directions.

Remember, the goal was usable Intel. But like I keep telling you, I was an amateur and a lot of what I did was nothing more than basic psychology. I was walking a psychological tightrope of an indeterminate length. I was still waiting for him to trust me, to bring me in. The reality was that it might never happen. He might never decide to trust me. He might choose, after having dealt with me, that my time on this earth was no longer needed. Perhaps I would end up as a caption in some obscure newspaper with little or no circulation.

Perhaps.

Then again, he was dealing with me, a Legionnaire, too dumb to know when I'm in way over my head, which I most certainly was.

One afternoon as the sun was starting to hide behind the high concrete walls, the concertina wire making jagged shadows across the concrete, he asked me something kind of spooky.

"Are you angry at them?"

"Who?" I replied without giving it much thought.

". . . The Americans."

I didn't answer right off. I let the words linger for a minute or two, pushing them out of the way as we walked back and forth. I studied this man. I glanced at the sky – looked down at the twisted metal shadows that seemed to be willing to cut me if I stepped on them. How did I get here? Who put me here? Am I alone?

And then after considering his question, I answered, "Yes."

THIRTEEN: My Militant friend

One thing that cannot be estimated by CIA analysts, hungry intelligence agents, or nervous lawyers, is the amount of time it takes for two people to develop trust and rapport with each another. Personalities are so complex – a mixture of nature (genetic predisposition) and nurture (what life does to an organism from the second it is born) – that attempts to predict the time frame and outcome of a personal relationship are incredibly inaccurate. Sometimes two people just hit it off.

Other times, they react like two bees in a glass jar, being constantly shaken until they decide to kill each other. With that, comes the reality that you can't assume that your spies will get close enough to their targets to produce reliable Intel. Psychological profiling may help narrow down the different options; it might shorten your list of potential agents for the particular operation.

But nothing more.

The rest is left to chance.

Over time, we began to share our histories with each other – all the tiny ones and zeros that made us who we were. It seemed like Nader would open up to me more and more each day. We would share various stories and details about our lives and with each came new insights into his personality – seemingly insignificant little bits of our lives that made us human. His life was a complicated mosaic. No longer was he just a monster or just a terrorist. In the same respect, I was no longer just a gun-for-hire. It was a slow process, but friendships are that way.

Yes, we were becoming friends.

You can't force it. Slowly, as each day went by, the suspicions and uncertainty seemed to wash off like the camouflage face paint we both used in the jungles to stay hidden. With each new piece of our former lives made available to the other, the walls of apprehension slowly lowered. We started to become more visible to the other.

I told Nader about my time in college, in Texas and how it cemented in me the resolve that I had to do something bigger, grander. I had to do something with my life that had an impact that was above the ordinary. Back when I was in college I didn't have a direction. I studied psychology and watched the sky, trying to imagine where my life would end up taking me. I wasn't a criminal back then. I wasn't a warrior. All I had was this strange, suffocating desire to do something grand. I could never respect myself if all I did was enter the corporate world and claw my way up to middle management, wearing one of those short-sleeved button-up shirts with a clip-on tie, or have some guy named Marty ask me about my notes from the staff meeting on recycling staples and paper clips – no, thanks. I mean, what would I tell my illegitimate grandchildren?

I had known for a long time, even before my days at UT, that I would follow the way of the gun. Maybe that makes me socially retarded, inept at living within the confines of a modern citizen's life. Perhaps I'm a bad American, not fitting the mold quite so succinctly. I am my own perfect nightmare. It is what it is.

Nader's story was much more interesting than mine. He had been advancing through the ranks in the Algerian Military. He was an intelligence officer and an Inspector, which he explained as a kind of intelligence detective who operates investigations inside and outside the military community. Trust me, those lines tend to blur. He was well connected, and I assume he was being groomed for much higher things. The government in Algeria is like a powder keg – so many secret groups all working for their own goals, trying to undermine each other. You can almost see the invisible strings being used by the French and American intelligence agencies (CIA, DST, etc.) manipulating the various players.

Unlike my disdain of an average life to drive me, Nader's decision to go against the system was due to murderous conspiracies and countless acts of anti-Muslim violence.

"All we wanted was an Arab government with the recognition of the Muslim faith and beliefs. If we have civil war, let us!"

He had to make the decision to turn against everything that he had previously loved and believed. Nader relived for me the phone call that he received, warning him that *they* were on their way to take him into custody. Interrogation was sure to follow. Its duration would probably be four or five days, and the end result would be that he suffered a heart attack (a chemically suppressed respiratory function), or some other irregularity during questioning. He would cease to exist. It would be just an accident, a hazard of the lifestyle. His family would not be compensated, and if they asked questions, they would probably meet the same fate as he had. His only choice was to run, and run quickly, because, they were coming!

He left the country within hours of that call, trying to cover his tracks the best he could in the short amount of time that he had at his disposal. Documents were burned, information was destroyed.

"Certainly they would have killed me," he said in his accented English. He had no option – perhaps if he had known sooner, or if he had a system in place for an escape – if he had expected their treachery – lots of what-ifs – plenty of maybes.

But all of it was speculation.

There were no concrete answers as we paced the warm concrete. As I listened to his story, I realized that he had no options. He was unprepared for the reality that his own government would turn against him.

In a lot of ways he was naive. For whatever reason, he felt safe in a nest of corruption. In an unstable government like that, everyone is somebody else's puppet. It was something that I, also, had to come to terms with. Although, in my case, it was not nearly the same scale. The flags of our fathers lose their luster when the thing you most believe in turns its back on you. It represents something completely different, something cold and distant, something lost.

After Nader's escape from Algeria he became a militant in every sense of the word. At that point he entered what we would call al Qaeda. He made his way to Afghanistan where he learned about fighting an uphill battle against the Russians. He practiced firing bullets and missiles, building bombs, and dropping helicopters out of the sky as if they were ducks at a shooting gallery. He learned the art of the ambush, and the art of psychological warfare. He continued on carrying the torch of Jihad, *the calling.* He operated in Bosnia, Egypt, France, Italy, Morocco, Spain, and eventually back in Algeria.

It must have been bittersweet as he secretly returned to his former home, at one point helping to develop a joint training camp for the mujahedeen and ETA (Basque Separatists who blow up cars and senators in Spain). This camp was outside the capital of Algeria, and it produced all kinds of dangerous men and women.

Within all of Nader's physical movements, you could see the echoes of war. You could see hurt and pain, an occasional wince, a slight pause in his breath, the careful way he slowly lowered himself into and out of a chair. He would limp a bit each day when we first started our walks. He had scars all over him – a bullet here, some shrapnel there. One of his field medics was probably Hannibal Lector. Different militaries throughout Europe and the Middle East had been taking shots at him for two decades. Along the way, he had taken some nasty hits. Close calls, as he put it, but he never felt sorry for himself.

"Not for one second will I apologize for doing the will of Allah. If I were to do that, I would be nothing, no better than a selfish animal."

He never felt sorry for himself. He never complained about his plight. If he didn't like something, he would be very clear in the reasons but never did it come across as whining. He had been forced to mature in his life much quicker than I had, and the realities surrounding him were much more life threatening. I had turned away from society because I didn't like where I was heading. Nader had turned away because they were coming to kill him.

Despite his religious beliefs and the violence that not only surrounded him but also seemed to radiate around him, I respected him as a person. He was a much more mentally tough individual than me. I figure that just about any man that met Nader would come away with the same feeling. To be able to throw everything away, over and over; to live without attachments, to pursue only that which propels you in the service of your beliefs – that is something which few people ever desire and even fewer accomplish.

Although he was smaller, and frail, and limped as he walked, and had been shot and blown-up, and was older than a soldier should be, he was the toughest human I've ever met. When you looked into his eyes and watched him speak, you knew, without fail, that he would not hesitate for a second. He had already dealt with many moral dilemmas that might have hampered a lesser terrorist. Like I said before , he was already dead.

When times get tough, as the bullets start to fly around you, your mind goes through something called the Boyd cycle. There are four parts to this cycle. First: Observation – you see the danger around you; Second: Orientation – you figure out where you fit in the picture; Third: Decision – you choose your course of action, your maneuver; and finally: Action – you make your move. The quicker that this cycle takes place, the more efficient you are in combat. Nader's cycle was instantaneous – a walking ghost following the path to God, not unafraid of death, but ambivalent to the concept. The journey that would lead him to salvation doesn't even give death a consideration. How do you stop a man like that? Kill him? You would just make a Martyr of him. He would become the stuff of legends and lore.

Imprison him? He will recruit from inside the prison and create a new breed of sleeker, more efficient assassins.

Appease him? How can we do that when we can't even make social security fiscally viable, we can't balance the budget, and we can't stop lying to our citizens as a general practice? Are we even mature enough to admit to ourselves that we haven't a clue how to win the *War on Terror*?

Change him? To accomplish that, you must understand why he is willing to die for what he believes, and we must be as willing to help him as we seem to be to kill him.

A man like that is unstoppable. The best chance you have is to get near him, to watch him, and to learn from him.

FOURTEEN: How to smuggle guns & cash

Throughout our conversations there was something that seemed to bubble just under the surface. It was an issue that we talked about rather indirectly but often. I got this feeling that he was trying to tell me without being direct about it. This quiet subject was the insertion of covert units and operatives inside the United States. Some use the term *sleepers.* The first logical question is that of finances. How do they do it? How do they survive under the radar for so long?

Let's talk about cash. You might say, *gee wiz, where do these terrorists get all their money?* Okay, petty rhetoric aside, it is very interesting the lines that get drawn back and forth across the Atlantic as we trace some of their money. Nader and I spoke often about finances. Though our conversations were more directed towards the safe harboring, procuring, and movement of such monies, there were occasions when specific information floated to the surface.

I had mentioned previously the Alkifah Refugee Center. Nader first brought the center to my attention when we were sitting on the pavement while the sun poured down on us from the Madrid sky. We talked about the different kinds of support that he had, and I inquired about American help. His posture hunched a bit as he spoke, and his voice was much quieter – almost at a whisper. He then outlined the nature of the Alkifah center.

The Alkifah Refugee Center was based out of Brooklyn, New York. It was explained that the real support for the Mujahedeen in America came from there. The cover was that it was this innocuous humanitarian aid organization.

It would be classified as a Non-Governmental Organization (NGO). There are all sorts of loopholes in taxes, accounting, and reporting that can easily be exploited by clever accountants working for such organizations, and that is what was being done. As far as anyone knew, this was just an aid group that happened to be Muslim. But it was, in fact, a much larger and more intricate set-up.

When I was in Spain with Nader, all I really knew was that money was funneled in and out of the United States through this facility. I was told that they had been doing this for some time, and that the accounts had grown to be very large, large enough that I was eventually told about an operation to procure a portable nuclear device. On television we always hear the term *Suitcase Nuke*, but that title is a bit misleading. They are not quite so small as to fit into a suitcase; however, they are small enough to fit into a hollowed out 36" television set. Luckily, such devices emanate Gamma-radiation that can be picked up by our FORTE (Fast On-board Recording/Reconnaissance of Transient Experiments) satellites. Such radiation must be kept under several feet of lead to insulate against particle emissions. So that's the good news: If they pull them out, we should be able to locate the general area within a few minutes.

Now for the bad news: The Former Soviet Union misplaced more than a dozen of them. Most likely some enterprising Russian Army officers got tired of being paid in Vodka and decided to try their hand at capitalism. I recently heard reports from a Russian officer who was assassinated in the late '90s. He claimed that the number of missing nuclear devices was over 80. Multiply 80 by a couple of kilotons a pop, and the result is an astounding amount of worldwide damage. We can't just blame the Russians either, because the United States has also 'lost possession' of at least two, and possibly as many as seven nuclear devices. So these little death boxes are floating around out there. It's just a matter of when one will be detonated.

Places like the Alkifah Refugee Center made the purchase of high-tech weapons and electronics a possibility. Perhaps Johnny Terrorist wants to bring down a plane at LAX. He contacts his handler, who then makes contact with the center. The finances are made available somewhere like Libya, Tunisia, or Algeria. A numbered bank account gets a mysterious infusion of a couple hundred thousand bucks and out of the darkness comes a Stinger missile. That little device then makes its journey across the pond in the back of a fruit container, or perhaps in a shipment of raw steel or lead ingots. Next stop . . . Mexico most likely, although any of the Central American countries will do. It's fairly easy to pay off a Honduran Customs official.

Besides, only about 5% of the cargo that enters a country is ever searched anyway, so it's a pretty good gamble that you could probably ship right through the docks without anyone raising a suspicious eye. A quick little trip through Mexico in a truck carrying old tires and trash, and the U.S. border is your last little hurdle. A Jeep at the front of the line gets popped with a pound of weed, and the next 40 cars and trucks go driving by while the guy in the tire truck winks at the Jeep's driver.

A month later, Johnny Terrorist is reading the instructions on the side of his Stinger missile while your plane prepares for takeoff. His eighth grade education doesn't hamper him, because there are idiot-proof drawings that are silk screened onto the side of the tube along with the instructions. Too bad for you that a senator, whose known to be an outspoken supporter of Muslim cleansing, happens to be riding in first class. The thing about all this is it came from Nader. It would be so simple that a child could do it. Kind of makes you feel all warm and safe, doesn't it?

Nader also gave me examples of how biological weapons could be smuggled in, but then he stopped halfway through the conversation and tilted his head back with a smile. When I asked him what he was thinking, he told me that you didn't even need to smuggle in a biological weapon – they're already here. All you need are competent engineers and scientists. All you have to do is put in a call and soon enough the Refugee Center will be making the connections for you. How'd you like an attack of Botulla, or Anthrax, or Cesium? Heck, you can pick up Cesium at almost every hospital in the United States. If they have X-ray machines, you're in the money – Botulla? – you can grow that on your own. It wouldn't take much to infect a city's water supply and within a week about half a million people would be dead, another million fighting for their lives.

I came to the realization that if anyone really wants to get us – we're hit. There's just no stopping it if the perpetrators are willing to die in the effort.

Part of the framework that makes all kinds of nasty things possible are organizations like the Alkifah center.

Now, I have done a bit of subsequent research on the Alkifah Center. The reason was that after I turned over this information to my attorney, I got news from Nader that the accounts had been frozen, and that they had lost several million dollars of 'aid' money. This was told to me only about a week or two after I passed on the name to my attorney. But there is a history behind the Alkifah Center.

At the height of the anti-Soviet conflict in Afghanistan, the U. S. set up a supply area in the rather dangerous town Peshawar. At the time, the CIA was backing a large rebel group of Mujahedeen. The leader of this group was none other than – Gulbuddin Hekmatyar. Many billions of dollars made their way from Saudi Arabia and from the U. S. and all kinds of weapons were delivered. In the middle of all of this was a Palestinian doctor named Sheikh Abdullah Azzam. He was one of the original founders of Islamic Jihad.

Azzam created the first center in Peshawar in the early '80s and it was called Alkifah. Over the next 10 or 15 years, he set up branches in different mosques in the United Kingdom, France, Germany, Norway, many different Middle Eastern locations, as well as the United States. It was known as Makhtab al-Khidimat (MAK), or the Services Office for the Mujahedeen.

The center that Nader told me about, in New York, was the flagship center in the U.S. It is located on the ground floor of the Al Farooq Mosque in Brooklyn. Other locations were opened in Tucson, Atlanta, Boston, Chicago, Pittsburgh, and several other cities. There were well over 30 different locations throughout the US.

In the mid-1980's Azzam was introduced to a young Saudi billionaire by the name of Osama Bin Laden. His family owned a large construction company and was delivering tons of equipment and machines. When they started building roads, caves, and tunnels, it was Bin Laden's equipment that did the bulk of the work. Later, Azzam convinced Bin Laden to become a financial supporter of his Alkifah Centers and other support organizations.

Azzam wanted to use funds primarily for the reconstruction of the government in Afghanistan. Bin Laden was pushing more towards a worldwide 'Jihad,' and eventually the two parted ways.

The rift escalated until November 24, 1989, when a car bomb in Peshawar exploded killing Azzam and his two sons.

I later learned through several news articles and related books, that the FBI had the Alkifah Center in Brooklyn under surveillance as early as 1989 after reports about a group of Arab men going to a shooting range and practicing together. This was one time where bigoted stereotyping might have been correct. If you were an aspiring young terrorist, then the place for you was Alkifah.

I must be clear on this; I did not know all of that background information while I was in Spain, I knew that it was important. I understood what kind of role it played in the overall Jihad effort. I knew that it was a freaking cash cow.

I'm still not sure what the exact moment was when Nader started to tell me things that were substantial.

Soldiers don't normally learn such information, because it makes them too dangerous if captured and interrogated. There's a point where your usefulness is outweighed by your knowledge of specific information. Ergo, you're better dead, where you can't talk, than alive where people can hook your ass up to a car battery and make you sing. The general rule is, keep 'em stupid.

I know there are tough-guys out there saying, "you could do whatever you want to me and I won't talk." Yeah, that sounds nice, but if I walk in the room with a jar of petroleum jelly and a rusted curling iron, you bet your ass you're about to talk.

Anyway, the kinds of things he was telling me weren't need-to-know information, at least not for the recruitment of another Jihadi, but as I later learned, I was not being prepped for a normal job.

Since my intelligence only ever went in one direction – from me to them I don't know what the government's opinion of the center was.

But what I took from all of that was: If the bad guys needed anything, money wasn't it. They had plenty. It was coming from right here in the United States. Now, one possibility was that Nader was giving me information that had already been compromised – the technique of *sharing without revealing.* He might have been trying to draw me in without exposing anything of real value. It is a standard intelligence technique, and Nader was a military trained intelligence officer long before he took up the cause of global Jihad. I believe that he wanted me to know things that could be verified. He had designs, and he wanted to make sure that I understood their capabilities – if only to frighten me.

Who buys the weapons that end up killing Americans?

Americans.

FIFTEEN: Where did the Missiles go?

As Nader and I learned more about each other and the motivating factors behind our lives, we began to ponder some of the edgier subjects. I remember a particular conversation that started about modern weapons and technology and evolved into a tactical discussion about guerrilla maneuvers.

My original stance was that sometimes technology is the deciding factor in a battle. I use the nuclear bombing of Hiroshima and Nagasaki as an example of how a new technology ended a major war. Nader, quite aptly pointed out Vietnam and Iraq. Well, one could argue that as far as the body count goes , the U.S. had dominated *both* conflicts.

But it's not just about the body count. America could never take from the Vietnamese the *will to fight*, and there doesn't seem to be any indication of the Iraqi insurgents laying down their arms any time soon.

Nader used the example of the fighting in Afghanistan to further illustrate his view. He explained that they were heavily out-gunned, out manned, and the technology was so far advanced of what they had that a head to head battle against the Russians would be suicide. "Suicide without a purpose is stupid."

"We would use the things which made them powerful to kill them," he explained. He told me that they had eventually received Stinger missiles from the Americans, but at first they were very limited in their weaponry. They had plenty of small arms and light artillery, but none of that was doing them any good, because they couldn't get close enough to use their weapons. So what they decided to do was play a game of cat and mouse. They would take the regular Russian soldiers and weapons out of the equation.

By engaging the Russians at unpredictable times and locations, they forced the use of more specialized troops. They would make the Russians chase them around the mountains, through the caves, in and around terrains that were difficult to navigate. They became formless and invisible. This frustrated the Russians to no end.

"You have to find us to fight us," he said as his eyes narrowed. "We would hide in the snow while a couple of our men would run out in the open. When the Russians would land their Special Forces (Spetznaz) in the large helicopters, we would wait with the rockets (RPGs, SA-7b Grails). You see, their large Helicopters could take direct hits from the missiles if their side doors were secured. But when the troops started to exit, we would rise up from the snow and fire on them with the missiles, directly inside the helicopter's troop compartment. Once the helicopter was destroyed, the rest of our men would begin with the Kalashnikovs (AK-47, 7.62 assault rifle)."

Now, this system may have been pre-Stinger tactics, because there isn't a helicopter that can withstand a direct hit from a Stinger. Perhaps the Mujahedeen were convinced by all kinds of propaganda that those Russian helicopters were indestructible, but I'm sure that after firing a couple Stingers, all of their previous doubts were cast aside. Again, these were simple farmers fighting against a far superior army and all the haunting reputation and stigma that naturally followed.

So then the Russians were scared to land their troops. They had to dumb down their strategies. And that further leveled the playing field. Piece by piece these nomadic farm people found a way to dismantle one of the largest and most advanced militaries in the world.

Sure, the Afghanis had aid money and weapons support, but they weren't flying F-16s and running Bradley fighting vehicles through the mountains. They simply refused to give up and found a way to best a larger and more advanced military using guerrilla fighting techniques. Like with the U.S. military presence in Vietnam, the Russians never could take away the Afghani people's *will to fight*.

You cannot beat an enemy like that. You either kill every last one of them or pick up your gear and go home. I couldn't really argue with what he was saying. Vietnam, Afghanistan, Algeria, Palestine, the Chechen Republic, the list goes on, and that's just in our time. Go back 2000 years: The Greeks, Persians, Mongols, British, Zulus, French, Russians, Americans. There is something about the "Warrior" tribal societies that drives them to find a way to win. A people whose backs are against the wall will always fight harder than those with options.

I wondered, as we talked about the sheer number of weapons the Mujahedeen had at their disposal, Where did all the missiles go? I asked him how many Stingers they received from the Americans. He estimated the number at somewhere around 15,000. To me, that number seems high. He may have been told that as part of his own people's propaganda or embellished a bit – but it is still daunting if even half that many Stingers made their way to Afghanistan.

So, then I wondered about how many of these man-portable shoulder fired weapons were still in Afghanistan.

"Oh, they are all gone now. We moved them."

"How many were left after the war in Afghanistan?" I asked.

He looked up and did some mental math, "Ten to twelve . . . uh, thousand."

Oh.

He then told me what happened to the remaining missiles. They had been boxed up for dispersal all over the Middle East. First stop – Kabul, Afghanistan. They were then moved in bundles to Egypt where they were loaded into several trucks. Then some of them headed west through Libya, while another batch headed into Western Europe. The trucks that headed through Libya towards Algeria had a little trouble with a Mig-29, but most of the Stingers made it safely into Algeria. Nader smiled to himself as he thought back. I believe it brought him great pride to constantly beat all attempts at undermining them. The other Stingers, the ones that headed into Western Europe are still available through arms dealers in Split, in the former Yugoslavia. So – they're out there to be had.

The reality is that those missiles could be anywhere now. Who really knows? Arms dealers don't take weekends and holidays off, neither do the *bad guys.* Remember: One man's militant is another man's freedom fighter, so the moral side of arms dealing never comes into play. War is good for everyone, at least – in the eyes of the arms dealers and weapons developers. Just ask the chairmen of Lockheed, General Dynamics, etc.

It's been twenty years, and I haven't heard about any large caches of Stinger missiles being found or used. So it stands to reason that they will pop up sometime in the near future.

I was no longer unsure about the capabilities of Nader and his compatriots. They had plenty of money and plenty of guns. They could get their hands on missiles and other explosives. They had the personnel to devise improvised biological weapons. They could travel. They could live frugally or extravagantly. They could fit in with our society, and we could not do so in theirs. if they ever wanted to get us, whether it be low-tech or high-tech – we couldn't stop them.

We started to become so comfortable with each other that I felt safe asking these kinds of questions. We were still discussing the Qur'an each day. I learned about the prophets, the Caliphate, and the tenets that were the foundation of the Muslim faith. Strangely, what I read in the Qur'an was not that much different from what I had read long ago when Christianity was being poured down my throat. The stories were almost identical. I didn't see 'kill the Americans' one time in the text. Religion was still not something for me, personally, but I tried to leave the door open. I wanted Nader to believe that I was convertible to the faith. He was under the impression that I had distaste for religion, and he was basically correct. But, he believed that I would become a Muslim if I saw it for what it really was. Hey, I'd worship the Frog God if that was what the job required.

Each day we talked about the Qur'an and each day Nader saw that I was more and more interested. He was clear that he didn't want me to convert to gain his approval, although there were several people around us in the unit that tried to do so. We would hear people yelling down from their windows, "Nader! Nader! I want to become a Muslim."

He would give them a polite smile and a nod, and we would continue walking. When we weren't facing them, Nader would tell me, "They only want to be Muslim because it is associated with violence in Media. For them it is fad. 'Jihad,' make a bomb, shoot machine gun!" Well, he did make it sound like fun.

One day we were resting because Nader's feet were aching. It was one of those warm, humid days, where you're always sticky and the air is thick. He looked across the yard at the large concrete wall and occasionally glanced at the razor wire above. "You know how to fight."

"Sure," I said. He wasn't really asking me, so much as just making the statement.

"You know all sorts of things about fighting that I don't know," he said softly. His head turned and his eyes met mine.

I searched the periphery and nobody was nearby. "Yeah, I know some things."

"Things you could teach," he said. "I have seen you working with Pasquale." He had seen me training our Italian friend in Brazilian Jiu-jitsu and some Thai kickboxing. We did it for a workout mostly but also to stay sharp. On occasion I had seen Nader watching us – and that was not an accident, it was by design.

"Sure. I could teach a group of guys to fight. I could bring them from the ground up: wrestling, striking, shooting, long-rifle, small unit tactics, basic small boat handling, VBSS This (Visit Board Search and Seizure). I know all sorts of things."

"How much time would it take to train a group?" he asked rather apprehensively.

"They already speak English?"

"Yes, they would."

I considered his question for a moment, did a few calculations in my head. "I'd need a place where we wouldn't be bothered for about four to six months. I'd need the equipment, guns, gear, stuff like that. Keep the groups small, no more than twenty men." I nodded to him. "But I could do it. No problem."

He sat back, his arms on the concrete supporting him as he looked up towards the sky, lost in thought.

He didn't say anything else about it that day. The next words he spoke were about the proper way to kill an animal for the purposes of eating. You have to sneak up on a camel, he said, or they'll start crying. I didn't know that camels could cry.

They're very clever, emotional creatures he explained. If you killed one in front of other camels, they will gang up on you in the future and try to stomp your head or bite you. For that reason, you must separate them from the others if you are to slaughter one for food. Apparently, those camels will hold a grudge forever. I guess camels are a lot like ex-girlfriends in that way.

I wasn't really sure if we were talking about camels, or if this was one of his metaphors, but then, sometimes a conversation is just a conversation. There doesn't always have to be some illusive, ulterior meaning. He was talking about vindictive camels. I was thinking about my short interview. Later, I would be offered a job from him, to work as an instructor at one of the Mujahedeen training camps that were being set up in Gambia and Laos. There was even talk of a camp in Mexico, but I think it was only speculation at that point. By now, as you're reading this, I'm sure something's been set in place. This was the job I was applying for.

It was a job that I wanted more than anything else in the world. I would, without a doubt, be deeper inside al Qaeda than any other American had ever been. The tactical significance of that is impossible to estimate. See, there are false-flags (double agents) all over the place. But to openly be an American, in my situation, and still slither my way inside the inner-workings of al Qaeda – that's an accomplishment.

We sat quietly as the clouds dragged across the sky like giant slugs leaving grey wetness in their wake. It's strange where life takes you. Who knows, somewhere back in America, my friends might be looking at the same sky, getting ready to head to the shopping mall, or to a bar, or to McDonalds for a quarter-pounder. I was infiltrating al Qaeda.

To each his own.

SIXTEEN: Real Intel is Ugly

Day by day, minute-by-minute, I was getting closer to Nader and his cause. We were talking about everything now. There were still questions that I hadn't asked him, but only because they hadn't arisen naturally in our conversations. He had made it clear that he would like to bring me on-board as an instructor at one of the training camps that were being set up for the new wave of terrorists in training. There was also something else that he wanted me to consider.

"I want to create an intelligence branch of the Mujahedeen within Salafia Jihad," he said as we sat outside slowly drinking small cups of coffee so strong that it could pull paint off of a car hood.

Salafia Jihad was the arm of al Qaeda that he was most involved in and devoted to. Roughly translated it would be, "the celebration of the prophets, teachings, and history, and the calling-to-arms to protect them." That was the way he had explained it to me anyway. He told me that his organization was comprised of very intelligent Mujahedeen who were very precise in their actions and operations and highly educated and goal oriented, mature men.

"We are part of al Qaeda, but we are much older with a longer history," he said as he sipped. "We must change and adapt as the world does." He smiled and shook his head. "Internet, computers, and cellular telephones that do everything...I am like a child again."

I asked, a bit shocked, "You don't have a computer?" What were next – no television, no radio, and no wheel?

"No, not yet – the brothers want me to get one so that we can make e-mails to each other, but I don't know where to begin."

I smiled, "My brother works in computers." I had an interesting idea pop into my mind.

"Really, your brother?"

"My real, I mean, my biological brother." I didn't skip a beat. "I can get you a computer."

"What do you mean?"

"I mean, I can get my brother to put together a computer for you. He can mail it to your house in Spain." He had told me about his place in the south of Spain.

"Would he . . . how much would it cost?" He wasn't asking because he was worried about the money. He had plenty of people who would provide money for him at the drop of a dime. He was just being business-like and polite.

I told him that it wouldn't cost him anything because my brother gets everything for next to nothing, and that they have spare computer parts just lying around. It would be a personal favor. He shook my hand with both of his; his eyes glowing like a kid on Christmas morning. He then gave me the actual address to his home in the south so that the computer could be delivered.

Later that night I called my attorney. I explained the situation that I had set up. My thinking was that surely the CIA could build a *special* computer that could be sent to Nader's home and used to monitor his actions. It would, of course, be doctored up so that any activities could be tracked, e-mails copied and sent to some unmarked office in Langley, Virginia.

Certainly we have this technology, and there is no way that the Intel guys would pass this opportunity up, right? – I mean, the ability to read al Qaeda's e-mail? Seemed like a good idea, fish in a barrel, a no-brainer.

So, several irons were in the fire – all sorts of potential opportunities to do some real Intel gathering. I knew that we were in. I say *we* because at that time I thought that I was part of a group effort with the might and muster of the U. S. Government behind me.

If things worked out right, we would have an American intelligence source at secret training camps in Africa or Central Asia. We would learn exactly who was communicating with the head of Salafia Jihad and ,in turn, who was contacting him. Since Nader had close ties to Bin Laden, it seemed like some kind of contact would eventually occur. Even from the prison he could send and receive messages in about four days. All of this Intel would be in real time once you had the ability to monitor his computer activity! Who knows what might come of Nader's idea to start an intelligence branch?

I have to admit; I was feeling pretty full of myself. What a fine little intelligence agent I had become. I'd like to thank the U.S. Navy, the French Foreign Legion, Robert Ludlum, and the U.S. Justice Department for indicting me. But seriously, I was proud of what I was doing, and I was doing it because I thought it was what an American is supposed to do in a situation like that.

I felt as though I was making up for my crimes by doing this work. You know, balancing out my Karma or something. I never asked for anything from the government. I was doing this because, in my mind, anyone who thinks that they can kill Americans and get away with it was sorely mistaken. I didn't care if I ever got anything in return for my service. It was enough that I had set out on a mission and accomplished it – and better than all those Harvard and Yale trained spooks.

The next morning we talked about his idea of an intelligence branch. It would be called the "Secret Group of al Qaeda." Ghaib Mujahedeen translates to the "unseen holy warriors." Over the next several days we talked about the formation and operations of this new group. There were several items of interest that we discussed.

This group would be younger and more socially capable. They must be able to fit in with modern society. They would be fashion conscious and aware of trends in culture and technology. They would all speak Arabic, French, English, and most likely Spanish - as the ability to function in Central and South America is now very important to a spy as well as any capable terrorist.

They would be adept at creating false documents to fit whatever situation arose. Usually they would travel under the auspices of the Press corp. They would be trained in the gathering of information and intelligence in all forms (cameras, computers, forensics, its interrogations, etc.) Their specialty would be the handling of after-action investigations, also referred to as postmortems. A cell might set off a device on Tuesday, and on Wednesday the intelligence branch would come in with the press and document everything – real, on the scene, usable intelligence that would be studied by men like Nader to better plan and prepare future strikes.

What, not scared yet? The other objective of this branch would be to carry out the assassination of individuals on the Fatwa (religious order) list. On that list were people who had so angered the Muslims that top-level priests had ordered the Fatwa of death. People like President Bush and all of his cabinet members were on this list. Enemies to all Muslims had a target on their heads. So this secret group would be well trained at close-quarters combat and all of the other dark skills that make a proficient assassin.

Let's take a look back in history. The original *assassins* evolved from inside the Nizari Ismaili Shiite sect during the 11th and 12th centuries. They were a secret group who would kill certain leaders who had tried to persecute the sect. They operated in complete secrecy. Anyone who had converted was held to silence, their allegiance hidden. The killings were well planned and strategic, but seemed sporadic to all but a few.

All of their enemies began to fear that they might be next.

Panic and fright spread like wild fire, and the paranoia started to infect all who opposed them. The strategic use of terror and violence that they perpetrated was one of the first organized terrorist campaigns for political power in history. Nobody felt safe.

In the dead of night or on a crowded street in broad daylight, they would strike. They could become anybody as they infiltrated every castle, organization, and gathering. When caught, they would blame others around them as being spies to create doubt and suspicion.

Their targets were uncertain whom they could trust. Even their own family members could have been infiltrated by these assassins. They were so successful that they brought an end to any pressures against the Ismaili Shiite sect. Everyone was afraid.

Now Nader was going to bring such an idea into the modern era. The Secret Group of al Qaeda was to be, now, what the assassins were nearly a thousand years ago.

How do you stop an assassin that you can't see? One who might be next to you at the airport, or in a line at the movie theater, or your bodyguard, or your kid's teacher?

– Perhaps a mailman delivering a letter?

– A priest?

– A police officer?

– A senator?

After a couple of years, how deep will this new group be entrenched? How many of them will have entered our society, their dangerous fingers silently waiting for the next strike?

Will they look like Terrorists?

Will they talk with an accent?

Will they stand over you as your wife delivers your child?

Will they watch as you bleed quietly out, fading into the darkness?

Will they lay a comforting hand on your shoulder as you cry?

Will you know if you are one of their enemies? Or will you just be an innocent bystander, caught in the blast?

In my opinion, this was going to be a very dangerous new addition to international terrorism. I stressed as much during my information dumps back to the U.S. I was worried about the possibilities of this group getting successfully developed – again.

But then – what do I know, right?

SEVENTEEN: Jihad, Southpark, and 9/11

Of all the conversations that Nader and I shared, there was one in particular which sticks out from the rest. The reason that it holds a special place in my mind, separate from our other discussions, is that it shook the foundation of some of my former beliefs – things, which, until that day, I thought, were certainties – things I could take for granted.

I tried to keep my ideas and views to myself through this entire operation. I didn't want to color the Intel that I was reporting, or bias the details in any particular way. The perfect spy would be nothing more than an information conduit; a human coaxial cable that takes noise and transmits it down a line without changing a single beep, buzz, or click. But we humans are relatively incapable of removing ourselves from our work – much like a photographer at a crime scene, snapping away photos of the grotesque from angles that he finds the most interesting and most telling of the horror. He thinks he is capturing reality, but he is also tainting it, skewing it for the next eye that will see those images. From then on, the reality of that scene is what is left on those photographs, but they are but echoes of the crime scene. That is the danger of human intelligence.

The spy must use everything in his arsenal to get close to the targets. He must be clever, cunning, smart and fast on his feet. He must bend and move like a reed in the wind, not fixed to anything solid, like the oak tree. For when the wind is becoming a hurricane, the reed will survive, but the oak will be uprooted and perish. The spy must do everything in his power to convince the target of his sincerity. Then, when all of that is done, he must step back mentally. He must become only a scribe, a simple human recording device. With all this being said, sometimes it is nearly impossible to stay on the sidelines when you are calling the game.

I remember that we were on one of our afternoon rec times.

I had been telling Nader about my opinion of a book that he had given me to read titled, *The Five Pillars of Islam*. It was early April, but for some reason it had become cold, as a blanket of anxious clouds ganged-up on the sun and bullied it into hiding. I recounted to him my ideas on the chapters I had read as the wind began to become aggressive. Gusts would plunge down around Nader and me, kicking up bits of paper and dust. There was this eerie whistle as the air sliced through the concertina wire. I could imagine the oxygen molecules being ripped apart by the razors' edges.

Without warning Nader decided to switch gears a bit. "Tell me about the fat one," he said rather anxiously. He was referring to an ongoing amusement of ours in which I would reenact different episodes of the show *Southpark*. You know, that terribly crude but funny cartoon with all of those little kids that swear all the time, hate everyone, and their feet don't move when they walk. He thought that my rendition of the different episodes was quite funny.

"Cartman," I answered.

"Yes, Cartman," he replied with a smile.

In many ways Nader could be just like a small, innocent child. I don't think that they had humor where he grew up. I think you are forced to become an adult at age six.

As I would recite the different scenes, Nader would laugh until he nearly cried. After several months of this, he knew all of the characters quite well. He could even do the voices; of course, he would never use any profanity. He liked Carman and Mr. Hanky (the piece of Christmas Poop) the most. It's always nice to share our American treasures abroad.

One time he asked me why we hated the Canadians so much.

The show frequently makes fun of our neighbors to the north. I said that we didn't hate them at all. Then he asked me why the cartoon makes fun of them all the time. I told him that I thought it was about being able to laugh at ourselves, since there is really no difference between Canadians and Americans. He didn't really understand, and I'm not sure that I did either, for that matter.

Perhaps his favorite episode was when Cartman was on his tricycle, acting like a police officer and giving people all sorts of guff. Nader would say, "You will respect my *authori-tye*," in his best Cartman voice, and then go into near convulsions laughing.

We joked around for a while and then we walked side by side, quietly in our thoughts, just the hum and howl of the wind as our background music. Strange, the things that bring people together.

As we walked, I considered all of the many things we had spoken of in our time together. There had been something that I had wanted to ask him for quite some time. But to do so, he had to believe that I had allegiance to him and not to the United States. It was a tense subject, but on that day – everything just felt right. We might have been the last two people on earth.

There is a lot of honesty in solitude.

We had just taken our shoes off, and it felt like we were removing the last barriers between us.

"You will be a good Muslim," Nader assured me softly.

I remained quiet for some seconds. "But I will be a soldier first."

"You can be both," he responded as he took my arm in his. "You *will* be."

I nodded. "I have a question . . ." This was something that had been on my mind for a long time

He waited for me to continue.

" . . . I don't understand the point of nine-eleven."

There was a pause, and he didn't seem to shift or change his posture in any perceivable way, but I could see him choosing his words carefully. It was as if he was preparing to explain something to a child, which I have kind of been on these matters.

"If I am in my country, and my people are waging a revolution against an oppressive government . . . let us do this. *Let* us. It is no business of anyone other than our people. If we start a civil war, what concern is it of the United States?" He looked at me, questioningly.

"None, I suppose. I mean, usually they do it for the sake of stability in the region," I answered.

"What stability? The United States supports corrupt governments all over the world. We try to revolt against our corrupt and evil government, and the U.S. supplies them with money and weapons to fight us." He let go of my arm as he continued.

"We appeal to the Americans and to the French or anyone else who will listen... let us have our war; but the world does not care to listen."

He stopped walking and turned to face me. The wind was strong enough that we had to squint at each other. "If, during your civil war, the Canadians would have joined one of the sides and killed your people, would you ignore this?"

"No," I replied. I hadn't really thought about it that way.

"Of course not. You would kill the Canadian soldiers. You might try to force them out of the country so that you could have your own civil war, but then what if they continue to support one side with weapons and money?"

It was one of those conversations where he pretty much kept talking and I pretty much kept listening.

"*Let us!*" "Let-us-have-our-wars!" he said, almost pleading to the sky. It was as if the swirling grey sky above us represented America – a large dominant force that would never go away; that would refuse to leave them alone. It was always there, watching their every move – waiting – plotting.

"If we talk to you, and you don't listen, and then we yell at you, and you don't listen, and then we show you the pictures of our dead, and you still do not listen . . . " Nader held up a warning finger, ". . . then you cannot complain when we resort to violence."

"The attacks of nine-eleven showed the Americans and the rest of the world, that even with all of their missiles, planes, satellites, bombs, and technology . . . that we can still bring them to their knees. Just look what a handful of people accomplished." He raised his hands to the side as if he was on the cross.

"And we could still do this . . . right now. *Nothing* has changed."

I agreed with him on that part. If five guys want to bring down a plane, right now, they can. If they're willing to die in the effort, there's just no stopping it. We walked for a while as I considered his words.

When he spoke again he was much calmer. "You see, the Americans need to let us be a country and go through all of our own problems. It is none of their business if we choose to live as Muslims. We are not asking them to change. We don't want their opinion."

I added, "I'm with you on that. They need to stop being the police of the World."

We walked slowly on. I was moving his thoughts around in my head, putting them in their appropriate locations for later retrieval. I will do that when new information is bombarding me. I try to relate certain things to key words or other hooks that I can use to get the Intel back out of my mind at a later date. But so far, everything we were talking about was ideology.

The mind of the terrorist or of the revolutionary – I'm not sure what is more fitting. I could see his point of view. We had no business, other than the oil business, interfering in the affairs of his and other countries in the Middle East. If we want the oil, we should just be honest with everybody and say, "*Hey, we're coming to take your oil!*"

But the world doesn't work like that anymore, does it?

There are no more Roman Empires or Khans. Now we support democracy, nation building, sowing the seeds of freedom, and capitalism. And really, I'm not sure that those things are really working all that well for us right now, not really working well for anyone.

Who are we, to assume that the American way of life is the correct way for the rest of the world? But then again – I wasn't there to study my own philosophy on life nor re-work my political beliefs. I was there only to get intelligence on terrorists and their future endeavors. I was looking for the kinds of things that I could pass along to much smarter people than myself who would fight these terrorists and the ideology that creates it.

"But the world looked at nine-eleven as a strike against innocent non-combatants. Civilians," I posed to him.

He nodded delicately, "Perhaps, but they are foolish people who sit idly by while their government continues to meddle in affairs that are none of their business and kill people halfway around the world . . . well those people are no longer innocent. Ignorance and inaction is no excuse. They call us terrorists because we use the only tactics that we have available to us, but who are the real terrorists? If we are . . . they are, too."

The lines do blur.

What he was saying made sense, and I could tell that he truly believed it. It wasn't just self-assuring propaganda. One man's terrorist is another man's freedom fighter. Surely, by the definition, the early American resistance that fought the British would be considered terrorists by most measures. We walked for a couple more minutes in silence. We watched this large butterfly get wind-shoved down into the yard, obviously separated from the path of her journey, lost from her flock. She was quite a contrast from the pale concrete with her white and orange splashes of color set against black wings. She looked tired and lost but determined. She did all sorts of busy little things with her little arms and antennae as Nader and I watched. She was gathering the strength to head back up again and pick a fight with the wind.

I could smell smoke drifting in from somewhere outside the prison. Then Nader said something odd. "Besides . . . the Americans let us do this." His tone seemed colder, more distant.

I glanced at him, turning briefly away from the butterfly.

"Huh?" I didn't get where he was going with that.

"Nine-eleven. Do you really think all of that could have happened if they were really trying to stop us?"

I shrugged. "Negligence, I guess. And like you said, five motivated guys can do just about anything."

"They let us do that," he said, never looking away from the butterfly. We stood there in silence as the dust etched our toes.

The butterfly finally took flight, making her way up and over the wall. I wondered if I had lost something as she disappeared into the abyss beyond the concrete walls that confined us. I was starting to think that maybe I was the naive one.

Was Nader saying that through negligence and apathy we Americans had let ourselves be attacked by men wielding box cutters? Or was he saying something much more sinister and frightening?

Was there an implication that the U.S. had been complicit in the 9/11 attacks – perhaps aiding or providing support to the hijackers? Or did the U.S. just stand by, waiting for 9/11 to happen so that they could easily pass legislation such as the Patriot Act and gain worldwide support for the War on Terror, a war which seems to only take us into countries with significant mineral and oil reserves – and opium.

I don't know, and I didn't much care. It doesn't really matter. All of it is so far over me that I am just lost in the shuffle. I'm just a human recording device. Obviously, my choices and decisions in life haven't been satisfactory, hence my being right here, right now. I'm not qualified to ponder stuff like this.

Just keep recording.

You know what? – it was none of my bloody business! I was a convenient spy, and by definition, I had no right to an opinion about anything. I am just a conduit; a piece of material being used by my government – the country that I still loved – the country that may or may not have loved me back.

I just kept telling myself that I didn't have, want, or need a point of view about any of this.

Do the job.

Keep recording.

Finish the op.

No second-guessing.

No hesitation.

If they had asked me to kill Nader, I would have. Not because I didn't like him, quite the contrary. I would rather do it than some stranger.

And besides, I owed my friend at least that much.

I am my own perfect nightmare.

EIGHTEEN: Smuggle the data

During the course of my intelligence gathering operation, I spent six months in the Spanish prison known as Madrid III, Valdemoro – Terrorist University. Of that six months, four were spent with Nader. I had been given a first-class education on terrorism. My eyes had been opened to just how dangerous and effective these men could be if provoked, and it seemed as if they had been.

In that time, I gathered 30 to 40 pages of handwritten notes. I had been continuing to make my information dumps over the non-secure phone lines to my attorney, but there were still so many little details that I had to preserve. There were obvious limits in a bunch of two and three-minute phone calls. It wouldn't do anybody much good if I lost everything I had learned over the last half-year, so I kept recording.

I stressed to my attorney that the intelligence guys needed to send somebody out to visit me so that I could pass on information to people who knew the political climate, and there's nobody more in tune with the Spanish pulse than the Company boys that were stationed at the embassy. He said that he would work on it.

I then asked him what the status was of getting Nader's new computer. He explained to me that the intelligence guys felt it was too expensive.

Too expensive?

The US Federal Government spends several billion dollars a day on nonsense.

I guess it would push the government over its spending limit to purchase a thousand-dollar computer. Isn't the national debt like two trillion dollars? I can't type zeroes fast enough to keep up with the growing debt.

So what's the difference? I mean, it's not like knowing *everything* that the leader of Salafia Jihad was doing would be important. I actually thought he was joking at first. Nope. A computer for Nader would be prohibitively expensive – all this from the government that paid five hundred bucks for hammers during the Iran/Contra operations.

I had heard things from Nader about something going down near us after the Hajj. He had said that it would be close to us, so I felt that there was a possible Spanish strike in the works. Upon hearing this, my attorney said that he would talk to the intelligence guys and see what could be done. Until then, he said to see if I could fight my extradition.

What?

He wanted me to fight extradition so I could stay longer in Spain, gathering Intel. He assured me that the intelligence guys he was talking to wanted the same. To me that sounded a bit dodgy because they had total control over my legal status and could make all kinds of things happen behind closed doors.

I called him a couple of days later, and he told me to change directions, *not* to fight extradition, but to now try to get back so that I could de-brief with the Naval Investigative Service, the State Department, and the Department of Homeland Security among others.

"So . . . now you *don't* want me to fight extradition?" I asked curiously.

"That's correct," my lawyer said, ". . . get back here as soon as possible." – as if I had some control over when I left Spain – as if all it took was a nod from me and the legal wheels would start to spin.

I laughed, "But two days ago you wanted me to stay–"

"I know, but ..."

I interrupted, "Well shouldn't you have this conversation with the intelligence guys? They could make a call and get anything they want done." We are talking about the same U.S. Government that is waging the *War on Terrorism,* right?

"I'm not sure it works that way. They're in different branches. See the AUSA (Assistant U. S. Attorney) is part of the Justice department. The intelligence guys can't interfere," my attorney explained, and it sounded dubious at best.

Really, it was absurd.

"I'm having difficulty believing that the War on Terror doesn't make a difference in a simple extradition case," I said.

"Yeah, but the AUSA is really being a roadblock," he said, almost sheepishly.

"Does the AUSA know what al Qaeda is? At some point somebody's got to step up to this guy and slap him back to reality. What difference do I make? I went to a gun show. I'm not some murderer on the run."

"I know that" he replied.

"Is the AUSA going to apologize when people start getting blown apart, or when A.Q. get a device?" My eyes scanned the area as I spoke, but nobody was near enough to hear me.

"Prosecutors don't think about things like that," he said.

"They want the conviction and the sentence. He's still mad at you for leaving. He was going to use you as his lead witness in the Murder-for-Hire case against Anthony. When you left, it made his case that much more difficult."

"The guy wanted me to lie under oath, and grass up everyone I ever used to be friends with . . ." I said, frustrated. Even as it was a shot at the AUSA, it was also a swing at my attorney, because he had advised me to testify against everyone. He said it was his duty as an *officer of the court.*

"I understand that," he came back.

"Well, then I don't get it," I said. "What you are telling me is that the United States Government's War on Terror can be temporarily suspended because some nobody AUSA got his feelings hurt. Something like that?"

There was a pause.

"Yeah, I guess it is kind of like that," he replied softly.

"That's stupid! – beyond stupid!"

"Well, yeah, it's kind of stupid. Look, we're doing everything we can. Maybe they'll just bring you back in a couple days, turn you around, and send you right back." That sounded stupid, too.

"Maybe," I said. I could just imagine my attorney sitting in his office slumped in his leather chair, shrugging noncommittally, not really appreciating the true gravity of my situation.

It was probably all sorts of fun to go to the bar and whisper to all of his friends that he was handling a spy inside al Qaeda, but it's a whole different animal when you're on the other side of the fence. On the inside it can be *unforgiving*.

"Ok, so what happens when Nader and his guys get free and start blowing stuff up? You know that they don't even have formal charges pending? Europe won't stand for a Gitmo (Guantanamo Bay, camp X-ray, Terrorist Detainee facility). They'll let these guys go any day." was my reply.

He didn't really know what to say. "We're going to do everything that we can." That's the typical lawyer answer when there are no answers, and you're about to get royally screwed.

"It's funny to me that I'm over here, in a hotbed of terrorists, and as far as I can tell, the only person holding a hostage is the assistant U.S. Attorney in Dallas, Texas. Doesn't that seem wrong to you? He couldn't even make his marriage work, and yet he's qualified to risk lives halfway across the world."

I knew that I was just venting now, but I needed the release. Complete idiots were poorly handling this whole thing, or so it seemed at the time.

"I believe that he'll soften up in time. He just needs his pound of flesh," my attorney assured me.

How about a pound of enriched Uranium? "Time is dead bodies over here. These guys are for real. This isn't a movie where you can press pause."

"We know, we know."

These are the same people that probably could have stopped 9/11.

"They're trying to get a nuclear device," I reminded him.

They were going to try to procure it through some dealers in Split, Yugoslavia, near the Italian border. The Mujahedeen had boats and money out of Greece that would aid in the procurement and relocation of said device.

"Nader's name isn't coming up on their (U.S. Intelligence) radar," my attorney said. Apparently the U.S. Intelligence guys couldn't find out anything about him . . . or at least, they claimed not to. I began to wonder if my attorney was being duped. Looking back, the answer is – *of course*.

"Well," I said, "their radar is broken. He was on TV next to Osama, so they've definitely got a file on him down here."

"Let me make some calls," was his reply.

"I'll call you in a couple days," I said, ending the call before I smashed the phone receiver into little bits on the wall.

Two days later I received a fax message from the U.S. embassy in Madrid. It informed me in Spanish that I would be leaving the country soon, and that when I left, I could only bring my legal documents and a pair of *court* clothes, but no personal belongings whatsoever.

This created a potential problem. I had all of these notes that I had been making for several months, and I could not bring them with me. I decided to take my notes and transcribe the key words and details onto the back of some of my legal papers. I figured that there was a good chance that they wouldn't scrutinize the papers too closely. But that was still going to be a risk. If for some reason the authorities took that paperwork or didn't allow me to bring it back to America, then I was going to be stuck. I needed redundancy.

An idea hit me. I went to my bag and pulled out my court clothes: a charcoal grey Dolce & Gabbana suit, and a bluish-grey dress shirt. I laid the clothes out on my bed and studied them for a few minutes.

I decided that they would be perfect.

Over the next couple of days Nader and I made our plans. I would go back to America and do whatever time I was required to do, and then I would return to Spain, and join Salafia Jihad. I would head out to one of the active training camps where I would begin teaching Jihadis. Nader would finance everything and make sure that I was taken care of.

"If all goes well, we will make the Hajj together, brother," Nader said.

He referred to me as one of the "brothers". It was the first time he had done that.

"Thank you, Nader," I said as we hugged each other. "Thanks for giving me a path . . . and a future."

"Insha'Allah, we will do many great things – many things." I handed him my C-bag with all sorts of stuff in it. There was a full set of camouflage fatigues, some jeans, some t-shirts and socks. "I want you to have my things."

He smiled as he took the bag. "I will hold them for you until we see each other again."

"Be careful, Nader," I said, knowing that at some point I might have to return. I might have to come back and deal with this dedicated, courageous, honest man.

A better man than I'll ever be.

I might have to return soon – *Return* – to kill my friend.

We looked at each other, quietly for several seconds. He shrugged, "What choice do we have, really?"

What choice did either of us *really* have?

None.

None at all.

NINETEEN: The sum total

I spent the next couple of days furiously consolidating my notes. I used the second and third pages of my Spanish court documents – the ones that I figured wouldn't be studied too closely if they were searched. On the backs of these pages I would transcribe my notes as small as I could, keeping most of it in chronological order.

I stretched, paced the room, and tried to put some of the more important details into my long-term memory. I also did my best to put everything I had learned into a kind of mental collage – sort of a sum-total for everything.

What was my objective?

To infiltrate al Qaeda.

Did I accomplish it?

On several levels, yes.

Did I obtain intelligence that could prevent or lessen the blow of future attacks?

I believed so.

Did I have the ability to continue my work in Spain or abroad?

Without a doubt.

So, it seemed as if I had enough Intel to be useful to the intelligence guys so that they could penetrate al Qaeda and Salafia Jihad. If my only use was to become an instructor at a terrorist training facility and be able to learn the location and identities of its students, it would still have been a valuable "get". I wasn't sure how they would use me, but I was sure that I would be used in some capacity. I already had more "in-the-field" experience and firsthand knowledge than many of the CIA's field agents ever receive. The reason isn't that I'm some kind of genius, but that I have the right credentials.

When I talked to a terrorist about fighting and the tactics of killing, it wasn't because I learned all about it in my field manuals, it's because I've done it.

I didn't allege to be a fighter – I was one. I didn't *pretend* to be a criminal, because I had become one. Believe it or not, there is a lot to be learned from doing some time in a prison; much the same as there are lessons to be learned from military service, which I had also done.

I've worked in bars, picked fights, and watched people die. I've traveled the world, dated models, wrecked sports cars, been successful, and lost it all. I've done the gig as a bodyguard, and also as a contractor hunting people who were surrounded by bodyguards. I've made mistakes, done stupid things, and chosen poorly on multiple occasions. I learned to speak French in the French Foreign Legion; I learned Spanish in Spain. I also learned a little Russian, a bit of Arabic.

"Learning a language is like having a weapon," a mercenary friend of mine used to say.

I've been shot at, stabbed, punched, kicked, and choked. I've been hunted. There is nothing quite so real as being hunted by other humans who want to kill you. It brings a proper balance to the things in your life that you thought were important. Colors become more pronounced, tastes more flavorful.

I've studied psychology, but not so much that I claim to know what everybody is always thinking. I've studied physics, but not so much that I quit staring up at the stars at night, or squinting at ghosts. I have learned when to stop and smell the roses, and also when to set them on fire for a quick diversion.

I like my chances in most situations. The odds don't usually bother me, but they do keep me honest. I'm not above a well-timed, tactical retreat. I basically try to do the things that people smarter than myself would do, and that makes me seem clever. Though in reality, I'm just a well-practiced impersonator – I am just as happy being me as I am being anyone else. I have no real identity, so I have no need to let my pride get me in trouble. You don't like me – whatever.

I don't care what people think about me.

I care what I think about myself, but I do have a moral code, something that I live by. I believe that people have a right to do whatever they please, but take responsibility once you do it. If you step on people then there is a chance that they will step on you in return. Don't cry when the music stops, and you don't have a chair.

People who prey off of those incapable of defending themselves, better not cross my path. If you do, you would do good to stay clear of my people and me. Oh yes, we mercenaries travel in packs, even if you can't pick all of us out of a crowd. Some of my best friends in the world spend most of their time behind a riflescope – watching you. If the job we're doing requires violence – stand by.

I like luxury and expensive things, but I don't have trouble being a cheap miser either. I will find a way to get the job done. I'm a big tipper, but if you spit in my food, I will turn your restaurant into the *Wild Bunch.*

I don't like to lose – at anything. My motto is, "You show me a good loser, and I'll show you a loser." For me, it's all life and death – every contest. On the battlefield or on a playground having a game of Tic-Tac-Toe, it doesn't make a difference to me. I'll turn a game of hopscotch into a bloodletting if I'm getting beat!

But above and beyond all of the things I have mentioned, that make me a good operator, there is one that rises atop all others. It is this: I know that I am not special.

There's nothing in my life that I can't walk away from. I just don't care that much anymore. People and stuff – they come and go. Nothing is permanent. The things in your life are like meals: some good, some bad, sometimes forgettable, sometimes beautiful. But soon, all that's left are some fading memories of what you had. That's it.

I realize that I'm not the smartest, or the quickest, or the most charismatic. I know and except the fact that I am very average in most things. Knowing all of that is what gives me the advantage. It lets me do the things that other people can't do, because they are too busy lying to themselves.

I know where I stand. That is what, in my opinion, makes a good operator in any environment. I was assuming that all those clever people behind the scenes during all of this would see that too.

The loud banging on the metal door to my cell was my alarm clock. "Nos vamos! Vas a ir por los Estados Unidos."

"Let's go! You are going to the United States."
I hurriedly put on my suit and gathered my legal papers – time to put on my game face.

"Listo?" the screw yelled.

Ready?

"Si," I replied calmly.

Yes.

They walked me to the bottom of the unit to the little room where I had been strip searched when I had first arrived. This would be my first test. The guard asked me to remove all of my clothes. Once I was naked ,he searched my clothes for contraband (keys, weapons, etc.) and then felt through my clothes. I acted nonchalant as he studied my dress shirt. Four minutes later I was on my way down a long corridor with guards on either side of me.

It seemed like one of those haunted house hallways that never ends. Though it was sunny outside, with bright little fingers of light poking through and touching the floor, it felt dark and endless inside the long passage. I was on the way to the receiving and discharge area.

It basically consisted of four large holding cells, the kind where the door was the entire wall. I was one of only two other people that would be leaving, and we all had our own holding cells. I flashed back to a memory of when I had first arrived at Valdemoro, being jammed into one of the holding cells because it was completely full. Prisons are a lot like roach motels in that more people arrive than depart.

I looked around, kind of taking it all in for one last time.

I could smell something like bleach but with a hint of orange in it. It made me remember that I was hungry and wished I had eaten this morning instead of cleaning my cell. I guess I didn't want to leave them any sense of who I was, the less in the way of a *footprint* or something.

Call it paranoia or whatever.

I waited for about an hour and then I was searched a second time. This time they were much more thorough, if you know what I'm angling at. The body cavity search came up clean. I put on my clothes and the screws handed me a big plastic bag with my watch, wallet, and cellular phone inside. I signed some release papers, and then I was marched out to a waiting van.

I arrived at what seemed to be a local Madrid Policia station about 20 minutes later. It was my first scenic view of Madrid. It's a very nice place to visit if you're not in prison.

At the station I was searched again and placed in another cell, alone. I spent the rest of the day and that night there. At around 4 or 5 am. I was taken out to another small van and then raced to the airport.

I had my papers, a plastic bag, and my clothes – so far, so good. When I entered the airport, I was taken through a back entrance and placed in a holding cell inside the airport in what seemed like a basement. Of all the places that I had been jailed, this was the one that I probably could have broken out of the easiest. But then, that was not my mission this time.

About an hour later, two chubby U.S. Marshall were leading me to a plane that would carry us across the Atlantic, stopover in Atlanta with continuing service to Dallas-Ft. Worth International Airport.

While we were in-flight one of the Marshals asked me if I thought that it was funny that the in-flight movie was *Catch Me if You Can*. I hadn't been around Americans in a long time, and I realized right then that we Americans are socially inept and rude. I could tell by the way the U.S. Marshals looked condescendingly upon everyone around them, as if the other people were some distance lower on the evolutionary ladder.

"Yes, I suppose that is kind of funny," I said as I sat back, trying to tune him out.

A Spanish flight attendant, who looked like a super model playing the part of a stewardess smiled at me and held up some food. One of the Marshals, obviously pissed that she didn't find him and his shaved clammy arms appealing, held up his open hand in the classic Stop*!* position. Then in his best *tex-mex* accent he said, "No pu-ede, no pu-ede."

He can't, he can't.

She shrugged at me apologetically and smiled the most perfect smile that I had ever seen. Of course, being in prison for the last six months probably skewed my perception a bit.

I sat back and relaxed. I'd let Leonardo DiCaprio take me halfway back to America. A few hours into the flight one of the Marshals – the one on my right – said something about Operation Iraqi Freedom.

"If you were still in the military, would you want to fight in Iraq?"

"It wouldn't really be up to me," I replied.

"They would force you to go," he asserted.

I didn't know what this guy was doing, trying to establish rapport, maybe? I don't think that this guy really understood much about the military, nor about war either. After I considered it for a moment, it kind of all hit me at once.

I was completely powerless. I had no control over anything in the entire world.

I owed nothing; I deserved nothing.

I was just a piece of damaged equipment, something that the government could dust off when the time was right, use me, and then put me away before the party starts, and all of the nice people arrive.

I turned my head slightly towards him and echoed something I had heard from Nader on one of our long walks, "You don't get to choose the war . . . the war chooses you."

TWENTY: Welcome home

Where I to be completely honest, I would say that my return to the United States was bittersweet. Essentially, the only reason I was happy to be back was so that I could deliver all of my Intel to all of those smart people who could accumulate, collate, and calculate.

Because of airline regulations, the U.S. Marshals were not allowed to place handcuffs on me during the flight, and they were not at all pleased with that. Once I was out of the airport in Dallas, the cuffs went on, and the tough guy antics ensued. I just kept my mouth shut and waited for another body search or two. I felt like a stripper. I had been searched five times in Spain: twice by the Spanish Prison authorities at Valdemoro, twice more by the Spanish Policia, and again by the U.S. Marshals.

By the way, they sent four Marshals to retrieve me from Spain. I had to wonder just how much money the taxpayers were getting bilked for that little vacation, round-trip tickets and accommodations for four men for at least a week. I assumed that they had a nice trip, because their eyes were bloodshot; they all had nice tans and looked tired and weary from nights spent masturbating to gay pornography or whatever it is four sad guys with deep seeded masculinity issues fighting off a mid-life crisis do while on vacation.

We left the airport, and it was late. They dropped me off at the Dallas County Jail, for the evening. I was unshaven, had a dark complexion and an overgrown drug-dealer haircut, and was wearing a 5,000-dollar suit. The people that were in my tank numbered about 40 and all assumed that I was a heavy coke dealer. I let them believe that. I ended up getting a nice place to lie down and about 15 job applications for bodyguards and street distributors. The next morning came quickly, and then I was picked-up and delivered to the Dallas Federal Courts Building.

I was led upstairs to a holding area with about eight small caged-in cells. One of the Marshals then led me into a small office where I was finger printed, and photographs were taken. I was, yet again, made to strip. This was my last hurdle.

While disrobing, the Marshall informed me that my attorney was here to visit me. I asked him if I could give all of the personal belongings to my attorney instead of mailing them home.

"Why not," he said, and he pulled out a large plastic bag.

He handed it to me and told me to get whatever I thought was important out and give it to my attorney. That's odd, I thought. There were supposed to be two bags: one with my personal effects, and another that was filled with legal documents that were to be given to the U.S. authorities.

I finished taking off my clothes, and the Marshall turned his back to the computer. I opened the plastic bag and found two smaller bags, each one having a note card with some Spanish writing taped to it. Luckily, they were both in a language that the

Marshall couldn't decipher. I reached my hand in and palmed the pieces of paper as if I was accepting a tip at a club, crushing them in my right hand as quietly as possible. I wasn't supposed to get both of these bags.

Inside one of the bags were my watch, necklace, cell phone, some keys, and my wallet – nothing super special there. But in the second bag: my passport, my French Foreign Legion military I.D., credit cards in my French name, and some court documents that I was probably not supposed to have.

"I guess," I said as I folded up my dress shirt, "that I'll just give all this to my attorney."

"Just throw it in that bag, and I'll give it to him in the visiting room," the Marshall said. He didn't seem to suspect anything. (Then again, why should he?)

Once the shirt was folded and safely inside of the bag, I tied a knot in the plastic bag and handed it to the Marshall. The visiting room was just down the hallway.

"Can I see my attorney now?" I asked.

"Sure," he said as I slipped back into my slacks and shoes.

I walked into the visiting room, which was no more than a square of about 10 by 10 feet, split down the middle with a metal screen. You could see the other person, but you couldn't touch them. That was probably a good idea because these were the rooms where angry people would come to meet their attorneys directly after being sentenced. More often than not, I imagine that most of the clients would love to put their hands around their attorneys' throats. So, it was an anti-strangulation screen.

There, in the middle, sitting across from the screen was Gary, my attorney. He looked about 20 pounds chubbier than when I had seen him last, (Lawyers!)

"How do you feel?" he asked politely.

I didn't really feel like a pleasant conversation, I was still in paranoid mode. "Did you get my stuff?" I said flatly. He nodded. He then lifted the bag up to a table where I could see it.

"Open it," I said quietly.

He untied my square knot.

"Ok."

"Now," I instructed him, "take out the dress shirt and the legal papers."

As he did so, he laid every article carefully down on the table as if it might be connected to a pressure switch on a bomb.

"Inside the legal documents you should find a bunch of notes . . ." I said carefully as he began to thumb through them. "Several pages should be there if they didn't find them. Even if they did, there are smaller notes printed on the backs of some of the extradition papers. It should all be there."

"I see some small handwriting," he said as he brought the paper closer and squinted.

"Good, now put that aside." He put the papers down beside the bag. "Now, unfold the dress shirt." He did. "Turn it inside-out."

He gave me a curious look, but continued. It was a little late in the game to become skeptical.

"Nice shirt," he said under his breath. As he had reversed the shirt, he saw the writing, "Oooh, look at . . . what is that?"

"That was my back-up plan." On the inside of the shirt were all of my notes, cataloged by major key words, and written in ink. Every name, address, date, and danger was copied. Both arms were covered, and almost every other available square inch of material on the front and back were covered.

The fabric was my tablet – simple, low-tech, and effective. It had passed through about seven different searches. If I had been trying to smuggle a spy camera, cassettes, or microfilm, it would have probably been discovered. Often though, the most low-tech, dumbed-down approach is the way to go. Nader reminded me of that.

Nader once told me a story about a how they used to ship weapons and money across the mountains. He said that it was too dangerous for the men to do, but the donkeys could be used. Once the donkeys had walked the path a couple of times, all they needed was the sound of a man urging them on. So they made a two-hour long recording of a man saying, "Hyah! Hyah!" Then they taped a Sony Walkman to the donkey; the headphones taped to his ears, and started the tape. A little slap on the backside, and off the donkey went. On the other side of the mountain the Mujahedeen would take off the shipment, put other stuff back on, flip the tape, and press "play", and back the donkey would go. Sounds stupid, works great.

Gary studied my notes, "This is a lot of stuff."

"Right. Now put it away, and make sure that it gets to the right people," I said.

"They are all quite interested in what you've got."

I didn't respond, but continued, "Now get out my wallet, cell phone, passport, and Legion I.D."

His eyebrows twisted strangely, "You're not supposed to have that stuff."

"I don't . . . you do," I said in a low voice.

"Now get that stuff to my dad, please." I might need it.

He turned his head from side to side as if somebody might be watching him through a pinhole in the wall. I rolled my eyes. I wonder if James Bond's attorney likes to play like he's a British Agent, too? Gary put my wallet, my passport, and my Legion I.D. into his jacket pocket and scooted closer to the screen.

"I don't know when, but soon Dave Watson from the Naval Investigative Service is going to interview you."

"Fine, but I only want to meet with him – nobody else. I don't know who anybody is, and I don't want to get burned. The more people who can identify me, the worse chance I have of staying alive back in Europe."

Gary nodded, but he didn't seem to appreciate the seriousness of the situation that I was in. There are spies everywhere – theirs and ours. If ten people saw me, then that's a whole bunch of people who might accidentally leak that I had been working for a U.S. Intelligence operation. That' s exponentially more chances that I end up on *Al Jazeera* getting my head cut off by a pruning knife.

There is a general law that applies to the security of secrets and information: It states that with each additional person that has access to information, the chances of a leak rise exponentially. So, one person is one chance for a leak. Two people equals four chances for compromise. Three people create 27 possible threats. See where this is going? Now imagine 10.

I only wanted to deal with one person. Then, if it all went pear-shaped – well, then I'd know who to visit.

After I met with my attorney, I was marched down in front of a Federal Judge who began to read off more indictments. I knew that none of them would stick because of the protection of the Extradition Treaty between Spain and the U.S. It was quite clear that the U.S. could only sentence me for the single crime of *felon in possession of a firearm,* the crime that I had been extradited for.

I had a bored smirk on my face as the judge said, "You have been indicted for *obstruction of justice, failure to appear, flight from prosecution . . .* " I guess one of the Marshals saw me not being sufficiently frightened and thought I was being disrespectful.

He barked at me, "Something funny to you?"

"Yup," I said with a grin, and then turned my attention back to the judge, ignoring him completely. I bet he was really angry – probably wanted to kick my ass. I felt all warm and fuzzy inside.

Welcome back to the United States, Mr. Huck.

TWENTY-ONE: Debriefing

The next day, per the Treaty on Extradition, the subsequent charges and indictments were dropped. I was carted off to a State and Federal detention center in Mansfield, Texas. I guess it was three or four weeks before I had the debriefing. It was quite a surprise – to put it lightly.

The first problem that I saw was that some of the information was time sensitive, and they had put off any meeting for almost a month. Why I wasn't interviewed instantly upon my arrival in Dallas, I will never know. Also, if I was going to return to Spain, things needed to happen to aid in my transition back inside. I needed to get the logistics and backstopping taken care of so that it wouldn't be quite so obvious. But on such things, I was in the minority.

When I arrived for the debriefing, I was shocked to be in a room with about seven or eight people not including my lawyer and myself. All of my notes were copied and stacked in a small pile on a rather large, wooden desk. As I entered the room, I noticed an FBI agent, Jim Christi. This would create a problem.

I remembered him because he had been one of the agents who had been investigating Anthony on my original case. I also remember him because he perjured himself during my initial bond hearing.

But, I was past holding a grudge.

What I wasn't past was a room full of people, one of them being a guy who already had made it clear he didn't like or trust me. A guy like that will run his mouth to the wrong people at the wrong time, and somebody like me will end up with nine grams of lead poisoning. In addition, Jim had wanted me to testify against all sorts of people, and that wasn't what the *War on Terror* was all about. No thanks, Jim. Your help will not be needed. Besides, he didn't have jurisdiction anyway. This was an international matter.

I was seated next to my attorney, and there were several other agents from the various intelligence agencies in the room. People were walking in and out of the room as if it was another day at the office. There was not even the slightest hint of security consciousness. None of these people would last a minute in the field. It was all just fun to play *secret agent* to them.

In front of me was Dave Watson, of the Naval Investigative Service. I was dressed in an orange prison suit, handcuffs still on my wrists, shackles still attached to my ankles, so there was a lot of trust being shared by everyone. Every person in the room was trying to look like the most important person in the room. I was starting to get embarrassed. Was this what U.S. Intelligence has become? – how far we fall.

I turned to Gary, "I thought we were clear about only talking to one person?"

My attorney just shrugged – one of those *my bad* kind of spineless shrugs, as if he had no choice in the matter. This was becoming a circus. I also realized that my attorney was no longer working for me. He was part of the machine. Just as we were about to begin, the AUSA Bill McMurray, from the original federal case, appeared to greet me.

Mr. McMurray squinted, eyeing me like I was street trash, "I don't know what's going on here, and it's none of my concern, but when you finish your Federal sentence, you will have forty-five days to leave the country before I come after you for aiding Anthony in the Murder for Hire conspiracy. You will have to find a host country that will accept you."

Then, the guy turns on the heels of his 12-dollar shoes and wheels on out like he just got elected president of the hair club for men. I bet he had looked forward to that moment for several years – practiced in the mirror and everything.

My attorney didn't say a word. He looked like he wanted to talk, but just couldn't find the right words. We call that being *in over your head*. Probably best, because when he did speak, it was incoherent and bumbling.

What went on for the next hour seemed almost surreal. They asked me questions, and when I answered, Jim barked at me. He would snap that they already knew everything that I was saying, and then he would protest that they didn't have any way to verify what I was saying. So, I was either correct – in which case they already knew what I was telling them – or I was wrong because they had no way to corroborate my findings. They claimed that they didn't know who Nader was nor had they heard of Salafia

Jihad. I thought that was a rather dubious position for them to take because Nader and the other AQ boys were being held at the request of the U.S. Government.

For every answer I gave, the reply was, "We already know that," or "That's not important to us." So I wasn't sure what they wanted me to say.

I decided against arguing. When you debate a room full of idiots, they don't realize that they're idiots, and you become one for trying. I just slid the pile of notes across the table to Dave Watson, the NIS guy. He nodded to me and took all of the notes. I also decided not to tell them about my *shirt.* Perhaps my back-up plan would be used for a different purpose. I didn't know what was really going on. Was I in the middle of a turf war between agencies or something less interesting? Was it possible that they thought I was making everything up? I guess that was possible except that we had been right about the Dutch Embassy bombing, and I also had verifiable Intel about several of the AQ boys. All of it could be checked. But then, I am a low-life criminal and am not to be trusted.

It was my impression that they were finding a way to write me off. They were going to ignore six months of intelligence gathering. I realized that we had learned nothing from the failures leading up to 9/11.

At any rate, Dave took my notes at the end of the meeting. He then told me in a lower voice that he would do what he could to get me signed on as an asset. (That's government speak for, an expendable agent who was not trained by the U.S. and therefore would be left out in the cold if things go tits-up.)

So the meeting ended, and I was sent back to the detention center.

I am sad to say, I was never interviewed again.

That night my attorney told me that they all believed that I was being opportunistic and withholding all at the same time. They thought that I was spoon-feeding them, trying to cut some deal to reduce my sentence.

"Opportunistic? I didn't ever ask for anything," I snapped.

"But you could have told them about the training camps and other stuff," my attorney said. Yes, it seemed as though he was on their side.

"I gave them Intel for six months at a pretty good personal risk and then handed them all of my notes. I haven't even seen that stuff in nearly a month ... what do they expect? And another thing, why was Jim Christi there? He has nothing to do with international terrorism."

"I'm not really sure why Jim was ..."

I interrupted, "And while we're on the subject, why was there more than one person there at all? Why was that debriefing done at the Federal Building where all kinds of people we don't know saw all of us in an office together?"

"That's how they do it," my attorney tried to explain. Now he was taking an accusatory tone with me.

"I risked my life in Ibiza and for six more months in Madrid. They asked me to do this, Gary. I didn't ask them for the privilege of infiltrating a terrorist organization. They came to me. This is being handled unprofessionally, and I am getting the feeling that you're on their side."

He didn't respond. We'll take that as a *yes*.

"I'll call you tomorrow," I said, and then I hung-up the phone.

The next day my attorney informed me of my next court date for sentencing. He told me that it was very important that I didn't say anything about what had happened in Spain. I was not to talk about anything that was discussed at the debriefing. I was to keep it shut. He assured me that the judge probably knew all about what happened, but that they didn't want it becoming a public affair. You know, keep it off the record for the good of the nation.

If you want me to clam-up just say it, but don't wave the flag in my face . . . it's insulting.

He told me that he had spoken to Dave Watson, and that my intelligence had checked-out. He didn't say, "Sorry for not believing in you," or "I should have listened more closely." No, none of that. He told me that they thought I was reliable again. They would all be working behind the scenes to get me back to Spain as quickly as possible. They needed eyes on Nader.

"It shouldn't take longer than six months, tops," he said on several occasions.

So, I did as I was told. I stood in front of Chief Judge A. Joe Fish and was quiet the entire time.

He asked me if I had anything to say that might affect my sentencing. I noticed my attorney nervously watching me, scared that I might suddenly talk. I said, "No, your Honor."

The judge then rambled on about enhancing my sentence from the original range of 41-46 months to a new range of 70-87 months. The reason for this was that I was being enhanced for several aggravating factors including: leadership role in the offense, the possession of five to seven guns, and obstruction of justice. All of that was in clear violation of the Extradition Treaty, but we didn't say anything – we, my attorney and I, just stood silent. Remember: My original charge was one (1) count of *felon in possession of a firearm*. That was all I had pled guilty to.

If the Judge had been informed about my circumstance in Spain, he sure had a good poker face, because we couldn't tell. In fact, he said, "I see no reason, based on your activities after pleading guilty, not to sentence you to the maximum that the guidelines will allow of 87 months."

And that was that.

I got sentenced to 7 years and 3 months in federal prison for going to a gun show while on state probation. That seemed to be more than just the *pound of flesh* that my attorney had promised me. It also seemed a lot higher than the six months he had spoken of so often. But, I was still being told that I was going to be inserted back into Spain to continue my work.

"Six months, tops." That was in September of 2003.

I informed my lawyer that we should appeal the sentence, and he seemed to agree, but said that he still believed what he was being told by intelligence agents. I think that he was a bit too trusting, because he never filed a notice of appeal in my case. Then again, perhaps it was I who was being too trusting of Gary.

Off I went to prison.

End of operation.

The funny part is that even after getting to prison, I was still being told by my attorney 'six months.' Gary still believed that I would be heading back to Spain any day, or at least he was telling me that to keep me passive and quiet. Looking back now, I believe that he was sincere. I think he was taking the government's word for everything . . . a rather naive and negligent position for a solicitor who supposedly understands Justice Department debauchery.

But, you know me and my blind patriotic foolishness. My dumb ass still thought that I was going back to Spain. I mean, how could they possibly overlook all of my Intel? How would they explain this oversight if things ever went down that could have been prevented? How would they answer the questions from the families of those future victims? But then, it's always been a government policy to just move on to the next story.

Could the U. S. Government, the Chief Judge, the NIS, the CIA, the State Department, the FBI, and everyone peripherally involved answer these questions:

Why did you let us die?

Why is our son dead?

Who let our daughter die?

Who killed our father?

Why did my mommy have to die?

Could this possibly have been prevented?

EPILOGUE: The failure formula

Within a couple of months, the realization that I was not important to the U.S. government finally set in. I was no longer on an intelligence operation trying to infiltrate al Qaeda – no more AQ breakfasts – no more Nader – no more "Secret Group of al Qaeda.," and no more Salafia Jihad – no more anything.)

I settled into prison life. It wasn't that much different from the Legion. My attorney created a memorandum that summed up what had occurred in Spain, and had it sent to Congressman Pete Sessions from Texas. His people deferred the matter to the FBI and tried to distance their office from any of it. I kept silent.

A petition for Pardon/Commutation of Sentence was sent to the U. S. Pardon attorney on my behalf. I was still in the process of fighting the legality of my enhancements by an appeal process known as § 2255. In 99% of all cases, the 2255 is either rejected or is not ruled on until the convicted person is done with his entire sentence. The pardon attorney wrote me a letter that said they would only present the President with my pardon application when all of my legal action was finished – which would be after I was out of prison, and it wouldn't do much good then. Dead end here, dead-end there. I stayed silent.

I was asked by my attorney to write down a couple of chapters about my experiences in Spain living with the terrorists and all that. He actually whispered to me during a phone conversation that he had *spoken* to some people in the literary field, and that there could be a substantial amount of money involved.

I still believed in my country. I still wanted to serve.

I remained silent.

I submitted a request to be able to return to military service and fight in Iraq. I figured they could use the help as they were having enough trouble convincing people to join the military when CNN was showing the daily body count alongside the high-definition carnage live from Iraq. You could almost taste the fear in everyone's mind. I received a nice letter back rejecting my request. I was getting punch drunk, and still, I did not talk.

The strange thing about a boxer is: he knows before it all begins that he is going to be hit the second the fight starts. He knows it will hurt, that it will be dangerous, and that it could damage him forever. And yet, he does it anyway. Most boxers don't ever get rich. They get broken and traumatized, but they still love the fight. They just don't have any other way. Even if you put them in a nice suit with a nice corner office, and a cute secretary with a nice voice, and a nice Volvo with good environmental friendly fuel economy – he would never be nice. He would never be happy. The boxer needs the fight in order to live, in order to feel a sense of purpose.

In the second week of March 2004, I was walking by the TV room on the way to my cell, and some people were crowding into the small room to see something. Like the rest of the sheep, I followed them in and watched as the photographs came in from Madrid, Spain, where there had been several train bombings.

I squeezed into the room and found a spot in the back corner. There were bodies all twisted and bent mixed with metal, rubber, blood, panic, tears, and . . . innocence.

The first reports that came in were assuming it was the work of ETA – *Euskadi Ta Askatasuna*, the Basque Separatists – but I knew that this had nothing to do with them. I sighed numbly to myself and then looked at my watch. March 11th, 2004. The Hajj pilgrimage had ended just two weeks ago. I didn't want to be right this time. I didn't want to believe that maybe I could have somehow made a difference. I didn't want to have been a good intelligence source – a good spy, or an asset. Not this time.

I just wanted to be a failure.

Over the next couple of days the information came rolling in.

There was a van.

There was a tape.

There were cell phones, residue and video images.

There were warnings.

Eventually, al Qaeda took responsibility for the attacks.

It was Salafia Jihad – the same Salafia Jihad, which I had been chosen to be a part of. It was the group that was led by my friend, led by Nader. The group I had infiltrated and which I could have been instrumental in understanding and dismantling.

I called Gary and he was going nuts. "You were right, you were exactly right! You called it almost nine months ago!"

"Now what?" I asked flatly. How many more had to die?

"They want you to go to work again!" he claimed.

"Set it up, Gary. I'll do it."

But that never came to fruition.

They said they were worried that I would just run again. They needed assurances and guarantees that I couldn't possibly give. All I had was my word.

I'd lost everything else. Again, as the dead were being counted and pieced together, the families being destroyed one phone call at a time – I remained without a voice, silent as a distant planet, as quiet as an old radio in some attic collecting dust.

Again, I continued my new life as a federal inmate.

In London, during July of 2005, several buses were bombed. The organization that eventually took responsibility was, "The Secret Group of al Qaeda." They had alleged ties with some of the Madrid bombing suspects and al Qaeda members. Well – of course they did. I didn't call my former attorney this time. What was the point? He just wanted to go on the interview circuit and get rich off of my mess. I started to feel sick to my stomach. I started to wonder if I was being a good patriot by being silent, or if I was an accomplice to mass murder. Had I become the very monster that Nader said he was trying to defeat? Or was I something much worse?

Was I being quiet because I was strong willed and patriotic, putting the greater good of national security above my personal well-being? Or was I staying silent because I didn't care any more? Was I scared to tell the story? What if nobody believed me? What if they retaliated against my family? What if they humiliated me? What if they tried to kill me? What if – ?

Then I realized that I, too, am a boxer. I am here on this earth for one purpose – to fight. All of us have a path that we choose among the myriad possibilities out there. Some of us become doctors; others aspire to build hospitals, some like civil service, others like food service. People sell shoes, and scientists design better rubber for the soles of shoes. People clean the air; others box it up and sell it. One way or another, everyone changes our perceptions of the world through their chosen path, good or bad.

I fight. It's the only thing that I do, and I do it in every aspect of my life. Whether it is chess, or in the jungle, or for the affection of a beautiful girl – I will fight. With a pistol or a pen, I fight. I will continue to do so. It is all that I can do. I can't stop fighting because I couldn't live with losing. It's more about me being a bad loser than anything else. You show me a good loser, I'll show you a loser.

For that reason I have chosen to not be silent.

I have decided to fight again. As sure as the setting of the sun, I know that this will be painful to everyone involved. I still have to do it. I'm ready for the character bashing. Matter of fact, I'll save them all a little time – I'm a bad guy. I'll carry a machine-gun for cash. I'll fight somebody else's war if the money is right. I'm no longer a patriot. I don't mind running up a credit card debt that I probably won't ever pay back. The last check I'll ever write will be to the mortician – and it's probably going to bounce.

Call me a monster.

I'm okay with that.

I have my own set of rules. Not your rules, most likely – but rules that keep me going. But I'm certainly not going to lie down, not on this one.

This is my fight.

 – My own perfect nightmare.

The fight is the only thing left which they cannot take from me even in death. But remember this: If you don't get me, you had better leave a light on late at night.

Now I am the Walking Ghost.

JAYDEN R. HUCK

UPDATE:

I think it's important for me to discuss a meeting I had recently with a former mercenary and friend of mine who was stationed in Iraq during and after the U.S. invasion. He told me that he had learned of a very disappointing situation. He admitted to me, with 100% certainty, that many of the kidnappings and video that appeared on Al Jazeera were actually conducted by contractors, pretending to be insurgents. He said that more often than not, it was *not* Al Qaeda dressed in a mask, but rather mercenaries that were tasked with reinforcing people's fear and anger . . . and thereby furthering support for the war on Terror.

It's something to think about when you watch those grainy videos. Another contractor, an old, rather salty operator once told me, "They eat their young," when referring to how intelligence operations typically play out.

After all, anything, no matter how despicable, can be rationalized by looking at the "big picture" whatever that is.

Thank you for purchasing my book. Please *REVIEW* this book on Amazon. I need your feedback to make the next version better. Thank you so much!

Check out my website where you can download all the evidence at www.TerroristUniversity.com

www.ingramcontent.com/pod-product-compliance
Lightning Source LLC
Chambersburg PA
CBHW070649290526
45790CB00001B/249